Advice From Strangers

Advice From Strangers

Everything I Know From People I Don't Know

RACHEL PARRIS

HODDER*studio*

First published in Great Britain in 2022 Hodder Studio
An Hachette UK company

1

Copyright © Rachel Parris 2022

A CIP catalogue record for this title is available from the British Library

Hardback ISBN 9781529372168
Trade Paperback ISBN 9781529372243
eBook ISBN 9781529372212

Typeset in Minion Pro by Manipal Technologies Limited

Printed and bound in Great Britain by Clays Ltd, Elcograf S.p.A.

Hodder & Stoughton policy is to use papers that are natural, renewable
and recyclable products and made from wood grown in sustainable forests.
The logging and manufacturing processes are expected to conform
to the environmental regulations of the country of origin.

Hodder & Stoughton Ltd
Carmelite House
50 Victoria Embankment
London EC4Y 0DZ

www.hodder-studio.com

To Marcus
You make-a mah dreams come true

Contents

Introduction

In 2017, I was invited by my old secondary school to be the guest of honour and give the all-important graduation speech to the assembled students and teachers at their annual prize-giving ceremony. When I was at the school, these speeches were a big deal – some of the last words of wisdom that these young women would receive before going off into the world – so to be asked to give it was both a great privilege and also an accurate description of most of my anxiety dreams.

I was surprised to be asked – when I received the email, I assumed it was one of the biggest administrative errors in the education system since Gavin Williamson was . . . born.

I was surprised to be asked, but not because I was a rebel at school, far from it. I worked very hard and was even one of those creeps who got on well with teachers. The. Worst. The most rebellious thing I ever did was get out of PE by saying I was practising for my Grade 8 piano . . . but I wasn't practising for my Grade 8 piano, I was practising for my Grade 7! Psych!

But no, I was surprised to be asked because in more recent years, the career that I presume got them to think I could give a good speech, is the same career where I talk about sex and depression and periods and angry politics, and I swear and I mention lots of things that aren't what I'd consider *school-appropriate*. 'How late in life can you be given a detention?' I wondered. And also, 'I wonder what detention is *like* . . .'

It was nice to be asked: an honour, a duty and, more importantly, quite the ego trip – the kind of validation a wannabe Leslie Knope like me can only dream of. And it was probably the last chance I would have to wear my prefect's badge in public.

1

So, I accepted.

And then I started to wonder what it really means to give a speech to send a class of young people out into the world. It should be powerful. It should be memorable. It should be useful. It shouldn't say fuck too many times. It should be . . . inspirational.

What the fuck would I say?

Well, as luck would have it, I had about a year to prepare, and in that year I would, as usual, be writing, previewing and performing a run of a new solo comedy show at the Edinburgh Festival, and then taking it on tour. Could I kill two birds with one inspirational stone? Use my show to help me write the speech and use the speech as inspiration for my show? Yes, I could!

The issue with writing a powerful, memorable, useful, inspirational speech for young people is that I am not a sage, an oracle or even, by most measures, a valid adult. At the time I was asked to do the speech, I was living in a small rented flatshare in south London, was a serially dating single woman in her thirties with no savings, no mortgage, no pension, no children, no living house plants and no washing machine. (I lived without a washing machine for eight years and I will never quite get used to having one now. I got so accustomed to handwashing my smalls in the bath like a Victorian and saving up other clothes for weeks and weeks for a bulk trip to the launderette, that I now find regularly 'putting a load on' to be an act of Dionysian-level indulgence.) No, my life wasn't exactly a beacon of success. What great advice did I have to offer to young women, based on my experience?

Very little, apart from how to get period stains out of knickers by hand (DM me).

So, in the tradition of *Who Wants To Be A Millionaire*, I decided to Ask The Audience. I took a comedy show on tour, and every night of it, for a year, I asked my audience, at the start of the show, to anonymously contribute their personal life advice for me, on little scraps of paper. I used their advice each night on tour, riffing off it in the standup and weaving it into an improvised song at the end of every show. But I also kept hold of these scraps, like a Channel 4 documentary hoarder, suspecting they would come in useful. They did.

This book is my response to some of those strangers' bits of advice. It's partly about me, partly about the world and partly about wiping your bum with a Tesco receipt. (See page 41.) It's purely personal and no doubt flawed in its understanding – the ramblings of a straight white woman who has neither studied sociology nor done a gap year where she found herself. (I don't know if I ever found myself, but I think the extent to which people think they have lost themselves is greatly exaggerated these days. We're all just *here*.)

I offer up this book in the spirit in which my audience offered up their advice to me: freely, in the hope it is useful to you, or that it, to quote a famous wardrobe-botherer, 'sparks joy'. If any of it offends or doesn't meet your expectations, I refer you to two of my favourite pieces of advice included in the collection:

'Realise we can all be a dick sometimes.'

And

'I am not a role model.'

I wrote this book during a very unusual time: through lockdown, through pregnancy, through grief. All times when I, when we, have desperately needed and wanted advice. Times of total uncertainty and fear and newness. Times when you look around for help, for support and for guidance. It's possible to find it in the least likely places.

I had hoped to mine the audience for inspiration, but, as I wrote this book, I realised that in fact they offered much more. These little scraps of paper offered snippets of the sad, the ecstatic, the surreal, the graphic, the genuinely sage-like wisdom that you usually only get from the likes of Maya Angelou or Dorothy Parker or Ru Paul. Not every bit of advice may have made it into that graduation speech, but I have kept them, photographed them and catalogued them, like the Grade A nerd I was at school, and like the treasures that I believe they are.

Never trust someone who when left alone with a tea cosy doesn't put it on his head

I agree, wholeheartedly. This was written by an audience member, has been famously coined by Billy Connolly, and is, in my opinion, a truth universally acknowledged.

This advice, at the heart of it, is about playfulness, curiosity and enthusiasm. Who really are you if you don't feel the urge to put a tea cosy on your head? It's begging to be attempted. Putting a tea cosy on your head isn't even a high yard measure of someone's playfulness, as I would argue the line between cosy and hat is very thin.* Most cosies are woollen, roughly head-sized and about the right shape – but *not quite*. And it's the *not quite* that makes you want to try it out.

You don't have to be a manic pixie dream girl who wears children's neon trainers and cuts your own fringe and dances like a robot to Nirvana, which you listen to on vinyl. I'm not trying to enforce false whimsy on everyone, but I do think there is joy to be had in trying things out – in laying your inner cynic at the door and being a bit silly. When you run out of wrapping paper, keep the long cardboard tube for a telescope to peer at other people in the household through. Rubber bands should be pinged at people. There aren't enough uses in life for them to get regularly used so give them a purpose – ping one right across the room at your niece. EVERY time you use a funnel, say, 'Now the fun'll start'. Say it with a raised eyebrow, to anyone in the vicinity or to yourself, under

---

* When you think about it, your average tea cosy is more hat-like than many hats. Hats are ridiculous. They've evolved from a basic way of warming your head into flat straw discs, vehicles for increasingly large bobbles or – the most absurd of all – fascinators. Think about Princess Beatrice's lobster hat: less like a hat than an actual lobster would be.

your breath. Never let a chance escape. See also: 'Well, this is depressing', every time you put the plunger down on a cafetière.

Putting a tea cosy on your head is like in that round 'Props' in *Whose Line Is It Anyway* where the improvisers are given a random object and have to invent scenarios where it makes sense. It's the same principle as all improv: it's just going, 'Hmm I wonder how this'll go' and then doing it to see. The most common fear that stops people trying out improv is the fear of looking silly. But in 15 years of watching, performing and teaching improv, the only people I've ever seen who really make you cringe are those who are trying to look cool. Somehow the people throwing themselves into the ring, trying and seeing, and having fun together, never look silly. Well, they look silly – we all look silly, but in a good way – in a way that draws you in and makes you want to join in.

My tribe, my besties, my gang, are the tea-cosy wearers. Those who, given the opportunity, will put a wig on a baby, will sing along without knowing the words, will 'try the grey stuff – it's delicious.' Just the quietly silly folk who like to try things out and find a bit of unexpected joy in the everyday.

Stay hydrated / respect women

This advice would make a great commercial slogan for a new 'women's water'. It's surely only a matter of time before Evian or Perrier catch up with the likes of Gillette, Bic, DulcoEase laxative and countless others who have created a 'feminine' version of their completely genderless product.

Other alternatives might have been:

'Evian. Live young – and ladies, look young.'

Or:

'Water for women – comes with a straw so you don't smudge your lipstick.'

This double-barrelled bit of advice also has all the hallmarks of a woman trying to smuggle her idea across the line at a board meeting by making it more palatable – in this case the most basic human necessity for life.

'Can we not have feminism this early in the morning, Jeanette?'

'Sure, well let's begin with just drinking water? And see where that . . . leads . . .'

. . . shortly before a male colleague repeats her idea about respecting women in a louder voice and everyone applauds him for it.

I can't disagree with staying hydrated – you really should. I mean, water is so boring; I do NOT like drinking it unless I'm already wildly dehydrated and that's the only circumstance in which it tastes good and you're like, 'Wow, water is amazing; I must drink it more often' and then you have another few sips and it's really boring again and you pour yourself a coffee. But yes, you need to stay hydrated. You'll die if you don't. You won't die from not respecting women.*

---

* But a woman might.

Unless the woman you're not respecting is, say, La Femme Nikita or Villanelle.

Respect women[*]

It sounds simple and obvious. Respect women. Of course you should respect women. You should drink water, you should brush your teeth, you should take care of your kids, you should respect women.

But it's not obvious, is it? It can't be that obvious because it doesn't happen all the time. 'Respect women' raises questions.

- *What* do we mean by respect? Doffing your cap at a lady or giving your colleague space to talk?
- *Which* women should we respect? Surely not all – terrorists? Murderers? Katie Hopkins?
- *Why* respect women? As a default? Have we earned it? Should we have to?
- *How* did Katie Hopkins get her own television show?
- *When* will it return to our screens?

Respect can be hard to pin down as a concept just as feminism can. Many more people call themselves feminists than I believe really are feminists, but I appreciate the gesture; I'd rather you felt inclined to say you are one, even if you're not. But here's what I think makes a feminist:

1. You think women are equal to men (not the same as, but equal).
2. You don't think that equality has been achieved yet (no, #MeToo hasn't gone too far and no, men are not being hard done by now and no, we haven't finished).

---

[*] This whole chapter is based around a few trending behaviours of men and women. I wish we lived in a world where I didn't have to put a footnote saying #NotAllMen but I fear we aren't there yet. So, yes, like with every issue, of course this doesn't apply to all men. But it applies to enough men for it to be a trend; behaviour that is widely recognisable is causing societal problems and needs addressing.

3. You want to DO something to make that equality happen. (Could be signing a petition, could be calling out male friends if they're sexist or you could be a full-on activist. But you've got to *do* something, you can't just *wish* it.)
4. An obvious one – You hate all men.*

Not everyone defines 'feminist' this way – just ask one of those sleazy guys hanging around in bars claiming to be a feminist just to pick up girls. So, if we have different definitions for feminist, then we also have different definitions for respect. If it meant the same to everyone, then it would be less of a problem to work out where you do and don't find it. If you asked the average man on the street if he respected his wife or his mother, he would almost certainly say yes, but if you asked him 'how' and 'in what way', he might have trouble.

The meaning of respecting women has changed. For many men, respecting a woman used to mean caring for her,† providing for her, complimenting her, holding the door open for her. It used to mean respecting her role as a mother or a wife and respecting her within the household. For many men, I think that kind of respect still holds true. Those men would probably say they do respect women, but I believe they respect them in a very limited way, in a very limited context.

Respecting women, as we understand it now, means respecting women on an equal footing with men. This might mean, for example, being as comfortable with having a woman as your boss as you would a man. It means trusting women when they write about politics/science/sport, as much as you would a man. It means not making assumptions about women based on their appearance or the way they dress any more so than you would a man. It means not sexualising women as a default. It also means acknowledging that their

---

* This is a joke! Obviously! This step is, in fact, entirely optional.
† There is a big difference between care and respect. You can care for someone without respecting them. I have cared for a pigeon I found in the road, but I don't know that I respect it.

sexuality isn't defined by you. It means respecting women's space and voice. It means respecting Black women as much as you would white women, old women as much as you would young women, mothers as much as childless women, poor women as much as rich women, women who enjoy sex as much as celibate women, women who you find attractive as much as women you don't.

You can't possibly respect all women just as you can't respect all men. We have 'respect your elders' trotted out sometimes too and I don't stand by that – after all, Dominic Raab is older than me. But perhaps Respect Your Elders is sometimes more of a reminder not to dismiss the older generation by thinking you know better. Similarly, I think by saying 'Respect Women' we're really saying, 'don't *not* respect women just because they're women', but that's far less catchy and would make a far inferior tattoo.

Like being a feminist, I think the best form of respect is an active one. It shouldn't just be something you have in your head, but something you show in the way you act – hence the phrase, 'show some respect'. Show it, otherwise what's the point?

Now, in approaching this chapter, I drafted out a list of ways in which the world at large can respect women more and that list of bullet points was three pages long. Just the list. That topic isn't just enough to fill a book, or three books, or a library, but several absurdly large libraries, all as big as the one in Disney's *Beauty and the Beast*. So, I have picked out just a very few topics here, but this is, of course, just the tip of the iceberg.

Some small ways in which you can show respect for women

Respect Our Space

On transport, in the street, in bars, in the park, in the workplace . . . There are a range of issues at stake here, let's start with an obvious one: 'manspreading'. The term 'manspreading' has become a bit of a joke – the cutesy word turns it instantly into a light-hearted issue – you imagine it written in comic sans and with a hand on a hip. It makes it bait for the anti-woke to go off on one:

'Oh, I suppose snowflake women can't even handle *knees* anymore; I suppose we men have to fold ourselves up into a ball do we, to satisfy the feminists? I'll chop my arms off while I'm at it, shall I? Oh, we can't even sit down right now – forgive me for breathing!'*

But the truth is, when some men opt to sit with their legs splayed so far apart that it encroaches on the sitting space of the person next to them, it is an insult. It says: 'My body is more important than yours. My comfort is more important than yours.' I've very often been the one squeezing to the opposite side of my seat, folding my legs up in a way I've never achieved in yoga, to accommodate a man's knees pressing against me and the infringement is unnecessary. There is plenty of room for the average man to sit with his legs apart on public transport seating, without sitting with his legs SO far apart they could park a smart car between their thighs. He may not be as 100% comfy as he is at home – sharing space on public transport isn't 100% comfy for anyone – but there's room for him to sit normally without crushing a 'nad.

So, why does manspreading still happen? Sometimes it's laziness, sometimes, it's trying to look butch and sometimes, occasionally, I think it's a conscious or unconscious power move. Men who do this, stop it. Be considerate. Don't make women sit awkwardly just so your balls can be strangers to each other.

You might say – well, why don't women just meet this with woman-spreading? Stretch their own legs out and press back against the

_____

* This is a fictional rant and frankly more mild than you'd find on much of Twitter.

unwanted knees of strangers? Sometimes they do but there are many reasons why not – if you're wearing a skirt or dress, that requires flashing your bits in a *Basic Instinct* kind of way which could raise another set of problems. It also requires touching the leg of a strange man for a prolonged journey, which, women know, is too big a risk to take. Sure, there's a chance the man will move his leg back to his own space, but also a chance he will take it as a come-on or, know it's not a come-on but nonetheless start to enjoy it. None of these are great options for women unless the knee-botherer happens to be the guy you've fancied for a year who works in your local Pret and keeps giving you free coffees. Generally, for women, initiating or maintaining physical contact with a strange man is a safety risk – that's why the girl to your side on the bus has only half a buttock on the seat and is holding onto the pole for support while you lounge as if you're at home on your lazyboy playing *The Last Of Us*. She's on the edge of her seat, staring ahead and uncomfortable, as if she was playing *The Last Of Us 2*.

You think it's a happy coincidence that she's chosen to sit like that while you've preferred to lounge widely. You don't think her position is dictated by yours. Maybe it is. Fellas – check your knees.

It's easy for men to claim not to know how much space women want or need – how can they know? Well, take a look at your average crowded bar area on a Friday night. Everyone's waiting for a drink, trying to get served – everyone's over-ordering as it's so busy, so every order is for at least 10 vodka redbulls and 24 shots. It is heaving. Impossible to allow personal space, right? No. Because if you want to see what an awareness of personal space looks like, observe how much space the average straight man gives to other men. Often guys are happy to press right up against women at a bar – to the front, to the side, but if they did the same to other men, they would expect a warning look or a bit of aggro.

In 2018, journalist Rachel Hewitt conducted a social experiment. Noting how much she had to duck and dive just to get down a crowded street without bumping into someone and observing that the majority of men she encountered seemed to make no such movements, she spent a month walking around without changing her course – the way she had witnessed many men doing. She reported that in that month,[1] she had only one collision with a female, while she had two or three collisions every day with men. She describes how she would stay on her course just as the approaching man would, and that she would watch as they saw her, clocked her and made no attempt to move from their course, and then become very angry at the ensuing collision – angry that *she* failed to move out of *their* way. Beth Breslaw conducted a similar experiment on the streets of New York in 2015,[2] with the same results: while most women cleared a path for her, she describes 'wave after wave of men knocking into her'.

This behaviour from men may not just be innate or subconscious but performed. A study by Jessica Nathanson reported in 2010[3] that they found not only this same trend of behaviour but that one of the men who was helping conduct the experiment who was trans, talked about 'learning that he had to walk down the middle of the sidewalk, through crowded spaces such as clubs, etc., with his head up, eyes directly ahead, without saying excuse me or worrying about bumping into people'. It raises questions of whether the habit of walking straight down the middle of the street without making way for anyone isn't just entitlement but, as Nathanson suggests, is also almost ritual – a performance by men and 'that NOT doing these things marks one as less than manly'.

I don't think men go out of their way to inconvenience women. I don't think the average man gets home and thinks, 'Ha! I made 35 women move out of my way on that walk – I WIN!' I think part of it is that the risk of collision is less important to men as, on average, they're less likely to be hurt by one or even notice that it happened. The men who do this aren't necessarily misogynists or chauvinists; they are simply, mostly, oblivious. But whether intentionally or not, as Hewitt says, 'Through an act as simple as walking, men stamp their power onto public space.' It's not a trauma, but it is a daily reality. Women are very used to making room on the street, and usually just get on with it, but there are times when you just want to scream 'SEE US!'

One more thing on personal space, and maybe this is just my bugbear, but please don't be fooled into thinking kissing women on the cheek isn't intimate. It is. You're kissing their face. Which is fine if you are close friends or family but not if you just met them at a work conference or you're buying a pram off them or something. If you aren't kissing my male colleague on the face, don't kiss me on the face, please. I know it's a social norm to many people – it's a safe move, no-one can call you out on it and it's thought of as best social practice by many middle-class men, but I, for one, hope it dies out, along with so much other faux-intimacy that living during a pandemic has successfully put an end to.

Kissing on the cheeks is common all over the world but in other countries and cultures it is less gendered – men kiss men on the cheek, or even mouth, once, twice, three times, depending on where you are and how drunk they are. But there's now a tradition – more in the south of the UK than the north, and more amongst the middle and upper classes, that you shake a *man's* hand, but you kiss a *woman's* cheek. Even when you've just met them! And it's a bit much, to be honest. I've had strangers or fans at comedy shows come up and kiss me on the cheek but shake a male comedian's hand. It feels too intimate, and I don't like it. It's odd, really, that the tradition suggests you can be more intimate with a woman you just met than you can with a man – it makes me long for the days of 1814 when unless you were family or a close friend, then you just walked into a room and curtseyed or bowed or moved your waist in one way or another as greeting.

I'm from the Midlands and where I grew up it was a simple code of Hug, Hand or Hello. Hugs for actual friends and family, handshakes

14

for formal greetings and just a simple 'Hello' for most other circumstances. The nice thing about Zoom meetings during Covid has been the de-gendering of greetings – it's been desperate inane hand-waving all round and I've enjoyed it. Don't get me wrong; I don't mind a bit of bodily contact but if you're kissing me on the cheek, I better see you doing it to the man next to me as well. Let us both endure/enjoy it.

Pay Women Equally
Pay women the same amount as men if they're doing the same job. Well . . . that's about it.

Let Women Communicate In Their Own Way
There's been a trend in recent years for telling women to stop apologising and being tentative in conversations.[4] There's even a downloadable Gmail plug-in called 'Just Not Sorry' that highlights how many times you apologise or use self-deprecating phrases in an email to help you sound more assertive. I definitely over-use 'No worries if not' in all kinds of situations:

'Shall we meet at 2.30? No worries if not!'
'Could you bring back some milk? No worries if not!'
'The Last Will and Testament of Rachel Parris: I bequeath my estate to be shared equally between my husband and any children issuing from the marriage, but no worries if not!'

Feminist articles have criticised women's over-use of the exclamation mark, over-use of 'sorry' and the way they add disclaimers to their contributions in meetings like 'if that makes sense' and 'just a thought'.

There are endless memes and guides that teach women to replace 'I'm sorry' with alternatives – particularly replacing 'sorry' with 'thank you'.* If you google 'thank you not sorry', you'll see what I mean; it's a whole phenomenon. The most common suggestion is that instead of saying 'sorry I'm late', you say 'thank you for waiting'.

And I'm not sure about this. Apologising properly, and in a timely way, is a very important skill to have – one that a lot of men in high positions don't have.

Which leads me to my bigger point – stop telling women to act more like men in the workplace.[5] The men you're aspiring to act like haven't necessarily got it right. 'You never hear a man apologise this many times in a day' – well, maybe, he should. Maybe he needs to. Perhaps men would benefit from saying 'no worries if not' sometimes and asking, after they've explained something, 'Does that make sense?' These phrases are thought of as more traditionally feminine speech patterns – more nurturing, flexible, even hesitant – and how great would the world be if more men valued those traits, and carried them into the workplace? I know a great many men who would benefit from a little hesitancy – a little doubt in what they've just said, because let's face it – sometimes it's absolute bollocks. A little more understanding, checking on the needs of those around them and, yes, apologising when appropriate, would go a long way. I'm not saying everyone should act like the most diffident person in the office, but neither should they aspire to act like the most assertive. Split the difference. Take a bit of assertiveness, a bit of politeness, an appropriate pinch of self-doubt, some caring what other people think and mix both humility AND inner strength, and you'll be closer to a happy workplace, happy household or, indeed, a happy country.

---

* This reminds me of a customer service training course I attended when I worked in a music shop. It instructed us to only ever deliver bad news 'in a good news sandwich'. It taught us how to learn when a customer is going 'into the red' (getting upset) and how to bring them back 'into the black' (naïvely trusting us). The course also told us that we should never say 'sorry'. Even if we had lost a customer's order, or charged them the wrong amount or accidentally recommended a MegaDeath record to a parent looking for sleepy time music. Never say 'sorry', just offer them an alternative solution. This was an American customer service training company and I'm sure influenced by the US fear of litigation – never admit culpability.

Did someone say Jacinda Ardern . . .? So, you can respect women by valuing different ways of communicating, not just demanding they strike a power pose and shout loudly to earn their place at the table.

Be Chivalrous, But To Everybody

'Chivalry' is a word that has historically been associated with the idea of respecting women, and what it is, ultimately, is men performing simple physical favours for women, who in return agree to sacrifice their autonomy. If you look up the dictionary definition of chivalry, it is still associated with a code of behaviour from medieval times, when men wore armour 24/7 and did a hell of a lot of killing while ladies wore, as I understand it, very tall pointy hats with gauze floating off the top and spent a lot of time in towers. Men could be warriors, kings or urchins and women could be damsels, queens or witches. It wasn't a great time for anyone – high death rates all round, not much infrastructure, unpredictable tax rates and a lot of that reedy folk music that gives you a migraine. But the concept of chivalry has somehow continued, even though nearly everything else has changed.

The problem with chivalry, or gallantry, is that it is gendered when it needn't be. There is absolutely nothing wrong with someone holding a door for a lady, but why would you not also hold a door for a man? If you really are doing it because of being generally helpful and kind, then why not offer that consideration to everyone? But note: simply holding a door to help someone is not the same as ostentatiously holding back a door, gesturing for a lady to go through while you hold it, making a woman squeeze past you, while you breathily mutter 'ladies first' and stare at her arse. Different vibe. When I hear stories from men complaining on Twitter that they got shouted at 'just for holding a door' and that's what feminism has come to now, I wonder if it was a scenario like the one above, and if they would behave the same way for a man or a child.

The same principle applies to offering someone a seat or offering to help with someone's shopping or carry a suitcase up the stairs. A good rule of thumb is: help someone who looks like they need help. It needn't be a move for or against feminism but just an act of basic human empathy. It is certainly true that it can be hard to read who needs help – and people are scared of offending – suggesting someone looks weaker than you, older than you or more pregnant than you, does run a risk of offending, I concede. But that's true irrelevant of gender and I suggest you take the risk. By and large I think people are glad and grateful for help; I know I always am. I'm considering launching a range of 'Baby On Board style' badges for public transport that offer alternatives like:

'Severe cramping occurring'
'Been at work for 12 hours'
'Surprisingly old'
'So drunk, might fall over'
'Hiding a panic attack too well'
'Gammy leg' or
simply, 'HELP ME'.

I spent ten years trudging around the London tube on the way to gigs, carrying a heavy keyboard and keyboard stand, and I wished, every journey, that someone would offer me help up the stairs with them or offer me a seat. Not because I'm a woman but because I was very obviously struggling with a load of heavy stuff. I needed a seat more in those years than I did while I was pregnant, but hey, it's not a competition. I'd have worn a HELP ME WITH MY YAMAHA SYNTH badge gladly.

There's also the issue of expecting something in return for, say, helping a woman with a suitcase. The reason a woman might refuse such help is that sometimes men expect something back. I don't mean a 'thank you', I mean, a favour, some attention, a conversation or a way of continuing contact. If you offer to carry a woman's

18

suitcase, *you* might not expect that but the guy before might have. So don't get overly cross with women if they say 'no' to help – there are several reasons why we might.

This is also true of paying the bill. I'm amazed that on programmes like *First Dates*, the staff, producers and editors still make a huge deal of whether the man will pay the bill – cue ominous music, close-ups of anxious faces and awkward exchanges. The absurdity of this idea becomes obvious when programmes like that have same sex couples on a date and the editors have no idea how to recreate that tension because they don't know who should pay the bill. Of course they don't, because it is arbitrary.

There is more than one issue at stake with someone paying your bill. One is risk – the aforementioned expectations; if you allow a man to buy you a drink or a meal, or a mega-yacht, there may or may not be an expectation of something back – ranging from a second date to a goodnight kiss, to sex, to a long term relationship.* So, allowing someone to pay for you can come with a hidden price.

This observation is ripe for a #NotAllMen response and can be met with total denial.

'There's no hidden agenda – I promise, I really just wanna buy you a drink! That's all!!'

I don't believe you. If I take that drink off the bar, don't say 'thank you', don't smile at you and walk off and continue having a great time with my friends, I don't believe you'll be content with that. So, I don't want you to buy me a drink.

---

* Like Stephen Cloobeck, a Las Vegas billionaire, who allegedly harassed and trolled OnlyFans pin-up model Stefanie Gurzanski, breaking a restraining order she took against him, after she broke up with him. He had spent up to a million dollars on her and according to her consequently would not accept the break-up or her continuing with her career on OnlyFans.

'Come on! . . . Hey! Hey! Come on, just take the drink; you don't even have to talk to me! What do you want? Hey! Have a drink?'

Perhaps he will leave me alone if I accept a drink. I take the drink.

'Well, you can at least say "thank you" . . .'

But I didn't want you to buy me a drink or engage with you at all, so I'm not grateful.

I say 'thank you'.

'What's your name?'

I really don't want to tell you my name. I don't want to talk to you. I just want to be left alone with my friends.

I ignore you, giving you an awkward smile to not seem rude or start anything. You take the smile as encouragement and come over. You're now next to me and expecting conversation. Now I'm in a position where I have to reject a stranger and it's certainly riskier and a hell of a lot more work after he's bought me a drink than it was before. I knew this was where it would end when you offered me a drink. That's why I said 'no'. I now hope you accept rejection without getting angry or not believing me and persisting.

'Stuck up cow.'

Sure, I'll take it, if it means you leave.

The 'at least say "thank you"' seems like it's a matter of manners but it's not. That man has forced you into a contract you never wanted to sign. You shouldn't be made to say 'thank you' for something you did not ask for, do not want and have already said 'no' to. That's not manners; it's coercion.

This shit is complicated and fraught with expectations that men might not even realise they have and with automatic risk assessments women might not even know they're making. Sometimes refusing a drink can cause more aggro than accepting one.

So when #NotAllMen say 'you can't even buy a lady a drink anymore', what they fail to realise is that it was never that simple. Buying a lady a drink has *always* come with terms and conditions for women – you're just now more aware of them, and you don't want to be.

Chatting people up isn't gone forever. Asking someone out isn't banned. Telling a woman she's beautiful won't land you in prison. These things will still happen and sometimes with lovely consequences. Flirting still exists; mutual attraction still exists. Making eyes at each other across a crowded room will still be the subject of love songs. But all those things now come with an awareness. We're all now more aware that those things can be more complicated than they seem and that there is always a power dynamic that matters. That's no bad thing. Romance isn't dead; it just takes a bit more consideration.

So again, this all comes down to respect. Women earn money. They know how to use it. Splitting the bill can set you off on useful, equal terms.

Jonny Chivalry: *'women today – you want 'Equality' but you still want me to pay the bill for you; don't you?'*

To which the answer is generally a resounding 'no'.

I have met a few men who confuse this idea of chivalry with the idea of romance. Now, I'm an old romantic. I love romance. I love candle-lit dinners, getting nicely dressed up for your partner, cosy nights in, thoughtful gifts, sweet little texts for no reason. But romance isn't one-sided. I do all those things for my partner and he does them back. Romance is a joint venture – if it's all one way then it starts to look either sad or sinister. So, no, I don't find someone paying my bill especially romantic.

Of course, if the deal is, 'I'll get this one – you get the next', then fine! That's equal! If they mean it. I might say 'great idea! I'll get the first – you get the next', and if they seem unhappy with that, then I'll know they didn't really intend to let me get the next. Or, quite possibly, the threat of a proposed second date has made them nauseous which I understand completely – I'm not for everyone.

Chivalry is what induced Jack from *Titanic* to let himself freeze to death in the icy waters of the Atlantic Ocean, just so that a woman he only met the day before didn't feel too crowded on the last remaining plank of wood. There was no need, but I hoped it made him feel good in those last few minutes. No, no, after you. Ladies first.

All this chivalry stuff is bound up in performative masculinity. When the guy on *First Dates* pays for the meal, it's not just to impress his date but also to meet the expectations of the waiter, the waitress, other diners and the production staff. When a guy gets a round of drinks for some ladies at a bar, he might well get an extra kick out of other men seeing him do it, and offering a lady a seat, while well-meaning, will always be partly driven by *looking* like a gentleman not just being one. Not all offers of chivalry are made with bad intent; this stuff is so deeply ingrained that when a man offers to pay for a lady's meal, he might really feel this is the right way for a man to behave. More to the point of the chapter, he might feel this is his way of respecting women. But there are far better ways.

At its essence, chivalry ought to be about showing respect for women, and if so, those men who claim they just want to be a 'gentleman', can chivalrously, shut up a bit in meetings and allow women's voices to be heard. They can chivalrously check if their female colleagues are receiving as much as them and act on it, if not. They can chivalrously share childcare more equally with their partners or chivalrously be a stay-at-home dad or chivalrously employ more women or chivalrously amplify women's voices.

Don't Slut-Shame

When I was about 23, I went on a European choral tour as a 'dep' or deputy singer in a professional choir. Stay with me; yes, this was my life. I was slightly older than most members and living more independently than many of them – having by then a job and a rented flat in London whereas many of them were still students and in the same social bubble. Bear with me, this difference is relevant to the story. While on the tour, two things happened: one of the boys in the choir, let's call him Bill, developed a crush on me, which I was made aware of, and I met a man from a different choir (it was an absolute choral bonanza going on in Poland that year) who I really liked, let's call him Ben. Bill with the crush was sweet, a bit puppyish and persistent. Following a night of everyone getting very drunk, he kissed me. I didn't really want him to but equally I didn't push him away immediately; I was sort of polite, I think, and very drunk. I walked away but overnight all the choir went into mad gossip mode, and I hated it. But the day after that I met this Ben. We clicked straight away and ended up having a lovely time together – he bought me flowers and we went on nice walks and made eyes at each other in the choir stalls – so wildly geeky but very nice. And great sex, frankly. Anyway, towards the end of the tour I was told that the choir I was with had a tradition of giving out funny tour awards in a little ceremony, and I was given the heads-up that I would be receiving 'Whore of the Tour'. I was pretty offended and defensive about this – I'd never really wanted to kiss Bill and my actual romance with Ben was none of anyone else's business. I thought I had made it clear to some of the people who were doing these awards: 'Look, I don't like it. I know you think it's funny but I don't know you very well and I feel uncomfortable. I think I'll feel really upset if you do this in public.' But the evening came and they announced me as Whore of the Tour and gave me a trophy and I had tears in my eyes with embarrassment but smiled anyway and left soon after.

Equally, a few years earlier, there was a girl at my uni who radiated confidence. She had sex with a few of the boys that I and my little group fancied, and we hugely resented her for it. Not just that she did it, but that she seemed so at ease with herself and so unconcerned about sex, compared to us with our myriad sexual hang-ups. And, simplest of all, we were jealous. We definitely called her names behind her back, simply because she had a fair bit of sex and seemed happy about it and fine with herself.

I've grown up a lot since then, but the moral of both these stories is – women can be horrible, including me, but also, we still live in a world where many people, including other women, judge a woman on her sexual choices, where they don't pass the same judgement on men.

On what terms do women respect other women? Sexual history is one of the factors on which men AND women can judge other women. But there are other factors at play. Do I respect the Kardashians for building up an extremely successful worldwide brand? Or do I disrespect them for promoting diet pills, bodyshapers and an unrealistic body image? I think I have a prejudice against women who have had very substantial amounts of plastic surgery. But why? Is it cheating somehow? Is it some primal feeling of competition for attention or is it more of an old-school feminist feeling that we should embrace our own bodies without adhering to the big lips, big tits and young girl looks of straight male fantasy? But I wear make-up, don't I? I colour my hair and emphasise my curves. I've worn bodyshapers and I absolutely intend to have botox so . . . it's all relative and impossible to justify under scrutiny. Respect from men will be a much harder fight if we women can't even respect each other.

I started writing this chapter enthusiastically, and to be honest, it has overwhelmed me. There is too much to say, too much to do. Most women are working very hard, not just doing the work of activism but, for many, simply living their lives. They are working hard to live. And we should respect that.

Respect is a slippery term. It's easy to claim you respect someone, but it is harder to show it. You can look at a given profession or a certain company or TV progamme* – its outward appearance, its representation – and it can look like women are equal now; we have done it – have a badge! Sit down for God's sake and enjoy it! Have a prosecco, love! Relax!

But we can't relax. Not while it is very very clear that society, by and large, doesn't respect women as much as men. That men don't respect women as much as men. And when you add into that being a Black woman, a poor woman, a gay woman, a trans woman, a disabled woman, a fat woman, then the problems only get bigger and harder to overcome. The mortality rates of Black mothers in the UK, the rise in domestic violence, laws against abortion, the continuing disparity in pay, the increase in incel communities, FGM, abysmal rape convictions; the evidence that we don't respect women is overwhelming and inarguable, and the consequences are life-threatening.

So, instead of listing all the things you can do to show your respect to women – that was genuinely my intention when I embarked on this chapter – I'm going to end on one suggestion: acknowledge that there's a problem.

Without that firmly, unequivocally, in place, none of the other stuff will work.

And after you've done that, offer me your seat please – I'm knackered.

---

* For example, the joyful *8 Out of 10 Cats Does Countdown* one-off special in 2020 where it was an all women panel. You conclude feminism has finished; we nailed it. But that would be overlooking every other episode, in which the regular comedians are nearly always straight white men. See also *Mock The Week*. See also *Would I Lie To You*. And *Have I Got News For You*. And *The Now Show*, *The News Quiz*, *Never Mind the Buzzcocks* (which, excitingly, was relaunched, hosted by . . . a straight white man!).

Acquire as many guinea pigs as possible – happiness will take care of itself

Hmmm . . . I've only ever had one guinea pig, and it didn't strike me as the kind of animal that would improve in high numbers. It was cute but provided very little in terms of entertainment, loyalty, playfulness or home security. It was called 'Guinea' – we were very bad at pet names in our house – so perhaps its absolute apathy was a reaction against us refusing to provide it with an identity. They don't give anything back, guinea pigs – they're all take, take, take, and the most they can offer you in return is reluctantly allowing you to hold them for a short amount of time, while they shake in horror, before they panic and flee.

Sorry, guinea pig lovers, I'm not an enemy of the 'pig', but I definitely wouldn't want to purchase them in bulk.

My opinion on pets is that generally it's quality not quantity. I think, for example, 'Tiger King' Joe Exotic's personality disintegrated the more tigers he accumulated. At one tiger, he was just a charming Florida eccentric, but by a hundred tigers, he was a raging murderous narcissist. Even on a smaller scale, I can never really trust someone who owns more than three cats.

I suppose it depends how big your home is. If you live in a small flat, don't get a pack of dogs. If you live on, say, a ranch, then I suppose you can get loads of animals, as long as you have time to take care of them. Horses, maybe? Cows, sheep, alpacas, perhaps – they're getting very popular.

But don't fill a 500-acre ranch with guinea pigs. They will cross the bridge from 'pet' to vermin quite quickly, and I doubt you'll have time to hold each one even once over the course of 20 years, and there's not much else to do with them apart from that. On the upside, if you *did* fill a ranch with pet guinea pigs, there's a good chance Netflix will make a cautionary documentary about you. So, if that prospect makes you happy – this advice is true.

A cup of tea really does make things better

If you like tea, at all, obviously this is true.

N.B. It doesn't make everything okay. It doesn't solve problems, unless your particular problem is a delicate balance of feeling thirsty and also a bit cold and in need of a mild charge of caffeine but not too much. Actually, as I'm writing that, I'm realising that is often my exact problem – I guess that's why *I* love tea so much.

Tea may not solve everything, but it might *help*. As the saying goes, 'don't let perfect be the enemy of good' – there is something about 'having a cuppa' that is comforting for the maker and the drinker, and it's not all about what's in your cup.

In the home, going through the routine of filling the kettle, switching it on, choosing a cup or mug, choosing the type of tea, getting the bag from the box and putting it in the mug, waiting for the kettle to boil, the steam, the click, the sound of the pour, the milk from the fridge, the sugar if you like – one spoon or two – the second wait – the brewing or too-long-stewing, the removal of the bag and the serving it to yourself or friends or the builders or your mum or your kid doing his schoolwork at the table, is in itself, soothing, normalising, refreshing. And then the third wait – waiting for the tea to cool enough to drink it – dividing the rubber-mouthed straight-away drinkers from the sit-it-out tepid tea lovers.

If someone is going through a difficult time and they offer to make you a cup of tea, it might be kinder to say 'yes' than 'no', thinking you're relieving them of a job. People in grief often need something to do, a job to put their hands to and also might be grateful to leave the room. Or just handing that person a cup of tea, with a taste and smell and object that is warm and familiar, is a start. A familiar ritual like making or drinking a cuppa can harness them, occupy them. Is it going to change their lives for the better? No. But might it be a very small anchor in a time of feeling out at sea? Possibly.

I think this idea can be applied to other small, useful actions as well, when people are in difficulty. There is a trend amongst the mental health community, and by that I basically mean everyone I know including me, for sharing memes and guides and explainers that list 'Things Not To Say To Someone With Mental Ill Health' or 'Eight Signs You Don't Understand Anxiety' and 'Nope, "Going For A Run" Didn't Cure My Depression'. These posts mock and condemn the actions of well-wishers who, when meeting with someone who's got, say, depression, try to suggest things that might be of any help like, going for a walk with them, getting outside, eating some nice food, using an app they've found helpful or even trying a craft or hobby that might occupy the mind from harmful thoughts for a short time.

I've experienced bad anxiety and depression, on and off, including one particularly long episode that I write about elsewhere in the book, during which I had regular panic attacks and stopped being able to eat. For me, there was anxiety around food and most food made me retch even as it approached my mouth, so I started losing weight as well as not getting the nutrients I needed to stay healthy, so my brain got worse and I went downhill.

I came out of it, with time and therapy and help from loved ones. But I do remember a particular point of help came when a good friend, who knew I was struggling to eat anything and who happens to know a hell of a lot about food and nutrition, texted me a smoothie recipe that included foods that are basically good for your body, your gut and your brain. It tasted nice and as I could drink it through a straw, I was able to have it without feeling sick or freaking out. And it was healthy. I remember the hour after having it was the best I'd felt for a week. My body had got a bit of what it needed and that made me feel better, and I felt better mentally. It didn't last forever but it was a good start. I also found an app that was really useful for controlling my panic attacks – catching them before they reached full strength and helping me with breathing and de-escalating it all.

That app, recommended by a friend, or that text from a mate about a smoothie is ripe for a mocking meme about misled do-gooders missing the point.

'Oh, you're depressed? Try this new smoothie, you'll bounce back!'

'Oh anxiety? There's an app for that!'

And that would be a shame. Because I believe these small things can help 'make things better' – not completely or permanently, but they can offer a boost, a moment of comfort or relief. I think it's important to remember that there isn't a huge divide between sufferers and non-sufferers anymore. Severity varies but I think we understand mental health enough now to see that nearly everyone suffers with poor mental health at some point and so, suggestions of help or advice are rarely coming from clueless outsiders, but rather people who have also felt depressed or anxious or lost or ill or in need of advice and who are trying to pass on a good deed. Telling those people they can only offer help in one exact way isn't good for anyone. The suggestions of help that are the most mocked are often the most practical and physical, as if those things can't possibly touch the edges of how we are feeling, but I think sometimes they can. I think we have to take very real, practical small steps to help ourselves. That's not to say everyone fully understands your inner experience, or how bad you feel; how could they? And there will always be people who downgrade it. But I think the vast majority of people who are making suggestions of help, not only mean well, but are worth listening to. Even if it's advice you've heard a lot before.

These things won't solve everything but maybe the much maligned 'going for a walk' might, today, make you feel 10% better for a while. Sunshine, endorphins, vitamin D, seeing strangers, thinking about something else, mindfulness, whether you subscribe more to the spiritual or the scientific there's a reason to think that these things might make you feel better for a while. Not cured, perhaps not even *great*, but a bit *better*.

So, if you are a tea-drinker, then yes, I really stand by this advice. That it can make things better. Whether it's . . .

A strong Barry's, a green matcha, a Rooibos or a chai,
an Earl Grey or a Tetleys or a cosy 'Sleepy Time',
a fruity number, fresh mint or a Russian Caravan,
or loose leaf or from Costa or an iced tea from a can,
or an Oolong or a barley or a Keep-Cup in the car,
from a fancy china cup to your basic mug of char,
whether taken in your Sunday best or in your oldest sweater
– a pour, a hold, a sip, a sigh – it really makes things better.

Never pass up the opportunity for a wee

As someone with a small bladder, I agree wholeheartedly, and my only caveat is that it's sometimes worth re-evaluating what you could view as an 'opportunity'. I have weed in a private carpark in the middle of Brixton, on a mountain top in a snow blizzard and into an Evian bottle in a tent at a music festival. And yes, it did spill.

I am quite a free wee-er – I'm not going around peeing on everything just for the sake of it, but if I'm desperate I don't feel overly embarrassed about finding a small group of trees or going behind a wall and hoping no-one sees, or, at least, that no-one really minds. And mostly they don't.

I think we are a bit precious about weeing in this country. Let me tell you a true story:

A friend of mine is in a weekly football team and they play on Clapham Common, where, ordinarily, there are changing rooms and toilets for those who have hired the pitch. But during lockdown in 2020, the changing rooms and toilets were closed. So, there was nowhere to pee as far as the eye could see, and they had an hour journey to get there, a two-hour session and then an hour journey home. So, she and a few of the women on her team went together to a bit of woodland on the Common, for a bit of privacy, to get changed and have a wee. They kept a look out for each other, for safety. A male park warden saw them, approached them and fined my friend £300 for weeing.

There are many ways you can be charged for weeing outside in the UK – the most common are either a PND – penalty notice for disorder, whereby you'll be fined £50 or £80 – or the various local authority by-laws about public urination, which is what my friend got hit with, which can be fineable up to £500.

To be clear – there was nowhere else to wee, she was being discreet, no-one else was around except her friends, and he fined her. There was no process of appeal; you just have to pay it, then and there. I think that is OUTRAGEOUS. Anyone at any time, could be:

- On their period and have an accident
- Pregnant or have given birth and need to pee urgently or indeed, have lost control of their bladder
- Have a UTI
- Be incontinent
- Have diarrhea
- Simply be desperate for a wee.

How can you punish someone for weeing in a wood? Honestly, what harm does it do the wood, and what harm might it do the person if held in? Sure, large amounts of urine are apparently not great for very young saplings or some flora and fauna, but I'm not talking about peeing on the displays at Kew Gardens here, just a one-off wazz in a field or dale. It only really harms the wildlife once '200,000 people pee everywhere' in the same local waterway, i.e., literally Glastonbury.[6]

I would have liked to have been the one challenged in that wood. I would have stood there, pulled my trousers up and visibly pissed my pants while eyeballing him, just to make the point. *This is what you're asking me to do, if I can't pee here.* Whenever I've popped into a pub or café, desperate to use their loo, asked very politely and been refused, I've wanted to stand there and bleed through my leggings just to make the stakes obvious. I've noticed that while heavily pregnant (or hot tip: crying), cafes let you use their toilets. But you shouldn't have to get knocked up to be granted some basic toilet compassion. Asking to use the toilet is rarely a casual question: hence the phrase 'I *need* to go to the toilet'. It is a *need*. If someone is asking to use your toilet, they are in need, and in many cases, it is urgent. They will, at least, be very uncomfortable if you say no. You're probably assuming they'll find somewhere else to pee, but if everyone says 'no' to them for the next half hour, they will be in pain, possibly wet themselves, possibly bleed into their clothes, possibly shit themselves. This is important. I've talked in another chapter about how #BeKind only works when applied to specific circumstances – well how about #BeKindLetPeopleUseTheToiletInYourPlaceOfWork. They literally do need a pot to piss in.*

So, yes, never pass up the opportunity to wee, but also let's *give* more opportunities to wee. And if you're passing my house and you need a wazz, my [toilet] door is always open. But . . . close it while you go, please; we're not animals.

---

* Possible addition: Keep a toilet brush and even bleach near the toilet and signage asking people to clean up after themselves. Not everyone will, of course, but some will. There have been times I've really wanted to clean the toilet after going (enough said) and there's been no brush to do so. At least give people the chance, and a little push, and it'll help out the person who cleans the loos at the end of the day.

Don't tell your friends about your Jane Austen sex fantasy

I don't think it was a coincidence that I was handed this advice and that I am in a long-running Jane Austen improv show. I think the author of this note has probably seen *Austentatious* and assumes I would empathise with them having Regency fantasies. I mean, I do. Obviously. But I have no problem telling my friends about it; I suspect that by creating a show where I get to dress up as an Austen character and act out entirely new romantic scenarios of my own making night after night, watched by hundreds of people, the proverbial cat is out of the bag, or reticule, if you prefer.

Jane Austen sex fantasies have been around a long time – we all know exactly what they were doing when they made Colin Firth emerge damply from a lake in 1995. That must seem very tame now that we have *Bridgerton* – where we actually get to see a duke and ingénue going at it hell for leather on a flight of marble stairs, which is a mixture of in-your-face-sexy and wildly impractical. There's a wealth of quality upholstery on offer – why not put a few cushions down at least?

I have no idea what this person's fantasy was, obviously. I wonder what it might entail. Perhaps something like this . . .

A brooding stranger arrives in town, riding a huge horse. He trots through the village of Oglethorpe, attracting gossip and rumour. He is handsome but visibly repressed. He has a twinkle in his eye. Eyes. For he has two. Two dark, troubled eyes.

It is Catherine's first season, and she is intimidated by all the expectations on her to catch a husband. Her family is poor, but

37

by chance and a great deal of luck, she is beautiful – like, pure knock-out. A stunner. She probably would've been 16 but for our contemporary fantasist to feel comfortable, let's say she's 18. She is naïve but clever – although not too clever – and terrible with money. She wears white dresses.

Her best friend, Elinor, is loud and funny and more confident in herself, and so less of a catch. She wears brightly coloured dresses and probably has red hair.

At the Partridge ball, all the eligible gentlemen flock to Catherine, enjoying her quiet diffidence and need for guidance. Meanwhile they laugh at Elinor's spirited conversation: 'She is almost as good company as a man!' exclaims one of the militia, generously. He would never consider her as a match.

There are hundreds of finely dressed aristocrats standing around looking haughty and dismissive in a posh, sensual way. One of them is a literal prince.

Across the room, the stranger in town from before, but no longer on a horse, looks on. His name is Sir Lord Fitz-Chesterton, and he spots young Catherine and strides towards her. He always strides. He is strident. He knocks over a couple of servants on the way, who apologise profusely. He arrives gallantly at her side, stepping slightly on her toe, to assert his strong physique.

'The first dance, Miss . . .?'

He expects her to say her name but she doesn't get it and just waits for him to finish his sentence before answering. He doesn't finish; he doesn't know what to do. It gets super awkward. He is staring at her, she is staring at him, the silence gets very long. During the silence, Elinor approaches them and asks if they would like a drink, thank God. Lord says yes, as does Catherine, and they all start doing shots, but shots of punch.

As they drink the punch, Catherine finds Lord staring at her with a mixture of arrogance and lust. Elinor is staring at her with a mixture of jealousy and lust. Meanwhile Catherine is staring at both of them with a mixture of innocence and lust, a combo which is very hard to read and ultimately cancels itself out. Catherine looks blank. Lord loves it.

By the end of the evening, the three are literally punch-drunk – but crucially, still in control of their decisions – and find themselves having to share a carriage home. Catherine's family went home without her because they have 17 daughters and forgot about her. Elinor has no family – she was a ward of a local dowager, which is why she is so fierce and independent. We don't know about Lord's family situation, but he sure is tall.

The chaise and four approaches and stops. Lord offers Catherine his hand to help her into the carriage and then Elinor gives Lord her hand to help him into the carriage. He doesn't need it, but he enjoys the touch of her palm.

As they sit in the cosy vestibule, Lord's elbow keeps brushing Catherine's waist, Catherine's thigh is pressed right against Elinor's and Elinor, frustrated by this slow pace, reaches out and puts her hand on—

You can find the rest of the story on my OnlyFans page for a small fee.

Check there's toilet roll first – Tesco receipts are very shiny

Here are some things I have used, in desperation, in lieu of toilet roll, in a public loo.

A Pret napkin
Receipts, various
An old, crumpled tissue
I've unfurled the empty toilet roll tube and torn it to expose rough, absorbent cardboard strips.
A scratchcard
A hair scrunchy
A deconstructed tampon
The edge of a paper bag
A page from a notebook
A glove
The lens cloth from glasses case
The paper you find stuffed inside new shoes
Bits of *Grazia*
Cinema tickets
A household bill

TESTIMONY NOT RECOMMENDATIONS. God help us.

Check your jeans have actual pockets before you buy them – not stupid fake pockets for women with invisible stuff

Most women's clothing doesn't have pockets. Trousers, jackets, skirts, dresses, shorts, novelty unicorn onesies; clothing that could easily accommodate pockets, doesn't. Some have embroidered lines that look like pockets but they're fake pockets. They're a piece of fabric and a button just sewn on top of the garment. Treacherous. Some have pockets that are so small that they are seemingly designed for women to carry around only the absolute essentials – a cocktail umbrella and a communion wafer.

Women's jeans have pockets so small they're about the right size to hold the bottom third of your iPhone, while provocatively showcasing the remaining two thirds to muggers: 'Go on, just take it; it's easy – it'll slide right out!'*

'But women's pockets are smaller because women are smaller.' Nice try but no. A study into women's and men's jeans showed that women's pockets on average are 48% shorter and 6.5% narrower.[7] Those shallow pockets would only be proportionate to hobbits. Most jean pockets for women aren't big enough for us to fit even our hands in, making 'looking casual', which surely is the prime purpose of jeans, very difficult. When you see a woman standing around with her fingertips determinedly squeezed into her jean

---

* Caroline Criado-Perez points out in *Invisible Women* that you can't fit an iPhone in most women's pockets, partly because the pockets are too small and partly because iPhone are too *big* – designed for a man's hands, not a woman's.

43

pockets, you are witnessing true commitment to nonchalance, and I'm here for it. But you shouldn't have to graze your fingers to perfect that buffalo stance.

I am a showbiz luvvie according to approx. 52% of Twitter, and true to form, I can boast that I have been on a red carpet twice in my life. That first time – the BAFTAs 2018 – what was more exciting than being shouted at by photographers and standing tantalisingly close to Bradley Walsh? What felt more liberating than removing my Spanx in the toilets just before the ceremony? I was wearing a gown with pockets. Big pockets. I posed for my first red carpet with my hands in my pockets and it felt great. No doubt this is why Olivia Colman copied me the year after at the Academy Awards – she's obsessed with me.

This pocket disparity is an age-old issue. In medieval times, a man and a woman, let's call them Osbert and Hilda, would keep their important stuff in bags tied round their waist on a girdle on the outside of their clothes. Then, after getting mugged for the thirtieth time that Whitsuntide, Osbert and Hilda started concealing their bags on the inside of their clothing, accessible by slits in their outerwear. But in the 17th century, men's clothing made the leap to sew those inner bags into the slit, creating the modern pocket. The same didn't happen for women.

From 14th century *hamondeys* to heavy, jewelled *chatelaines*, from Regency reticules to Gucci leather handbags and the 65 canvas tote bags I currently keep in circulation, women have always had to carry bags where men have not.

I've never been a fan of the handbag. If it's on your shoulder it either weighs you down or falls off. If you're carrying it in your hand, you are minus one functioning hand – it makes you less able to easily, quickly act. You can't suddenly join a flashmob or heroically save a toddler from scooting into a six-lane motorway or just hold a Costa coffee AND a muffin. The handbag is cumbersome. It slows women down.

It was from the late 18th century that women stopped carrying bags under their skirts. The fashion didn't allow for it; it was more important that a woman's figure not be compromised than she have the ability to carry her stuff easily.

The same principles hold today:
- that pockets would compromise the line of an outfit and that a woman's figure is more important
- that women like carrying handbags
- that women have either nothing to carry around or have such a wealth of mysterious feminine stuff that it wouldn't fit in a pocket.

The first wave feminists in the late 19th century knew what a lack of pockets represented. The Rational Dress Movement got rid of boned corsets in favour of healthier, more practical and more comfortable options for women – loose trousers and bloomers that allowed for more movement, like cycling, and plenty of pockets.

The Suffragette Suit of 1910 was designed to accommodate the growing number of women wanting more comfort, move-ment and, frankly, storage. They had seven or eight pockets in a suit, 'all in sight and easy to find'. Even in formal wear, women were challenging the norm: Gail Laughlin, an activist for women's rights and lawyer, refused to wear an evening gown until pockets were sewn in.

An 1899 *New York Times* piece makes the somewhat tongue-in-cheek claim that civilisation itself is founded on pockets.[8] 'As we become more civilised, we need more pockets,' the piece says. 'No pocketless people has ever been great since pockets were invented, and the female sex cannot rival us while it is pocketless.'

There was a panic about not just what women might store in their pockets but also the general stance and demeanour of women standing with their hands in their pockets. What would become of their 'blushes, shyness and embarrassment'?* God forbid that women were relaxed and confident. I know when I created my eHarmony profile, I included that 'I blush, I am shy and best of all, I am constantly embarrassed'. I was very popular. At the turn of the 20th century, the image of a woman strolling with ease, hands in pockets down a street was enough to send some people into hysterical paroxysms, ironically. If only they'd known that 100 years later, pockets in women's clothing would still be rare OR so small that if they did attempt to put their hands in them, strolling down the street would only be possible by adopting a constricted walk reminiscent of a newborn giraffe.

Here I feel I have to point out, that some women really love their bags. I'm not going to war with bags. Sometimes we need to carry more than you could ever fit in a pocket. But so do men. And when men have the occasion to carry a bag, it's so unusual that it gets called a 'manbag'. The concept of having to employ an extraneous receptacle to carry your belongings from one place to another is so unique to the feminine experience that a man doing it requires a special label. This practice is ridiculous but quite funny. Guy-liner, mansturiser, the desperate terms that help society accommodate men doing anything a woman ever did are luckily ridiculous enough to be placed under 'humour' instead of 'heteronormative bullshit'.

Most men's clothes have pockets. This makes their lives a bit easier. Let us assume women would welcome the same opportunity. Actually, we don't have to assume – we have the research.⁹ Women

---

* 'The pockets of the 'New Woman,' admirably useful as they are, seem likely to prove her new fetish, to stand her instead of blushes and shyness and embarrassment, for who can be any of these things while she stands with her hands in her pockets?' – *The Graphic* 1894

do. When we have pockets, we will have more ready hands, more useful bodies and more of our cool shit easily to hand, whether that's a glue-gun or a multi-tool. And we'll have the answers to the big questions like:

'Is that a banana in your pocket or are you just pleased to se—'
'YES! It's a banana! In my pocket! I can fit a whole banana in my pocket, the pocket I have! Imagine that! In MY pocket! A banana! What dreams may come . . .'

Middle Class Advice #27: Consume macaron(s) immediately after purchase, lest they become dust

There were some pieces of advice where it was more the imagined author, than the advice, that made a lasting impression. I love this. I so wish I knew who wrote this. The mild self-deprecation. The hesitant plural. 'Lest'. This is how I imagine you. You are British but you were educated at international schools because your parents are European diplomats. You enjoy poetry – particularly the lake poets, but also Rumi. You now live mostly in Paris; you moved there because you fell in love with a girl who was studying at Le Coq but soon discovered she was too much like her mask – always moving onto the next thing and the next – while you wanted to find a place in this world and stop moving, at last. You have inherited wealth, but it is in a trust that you neither use nor want and has sat untouched for many years since you found out about it. You buy your macaron(s) in Paris but not at Ladurée – you know where the best places are. You love all kinds of comedy – you come to the Edinburgh Fringe every year for a few days and try new faces as well as familiar names. By profession, you are a tailor. You learnt your craft on Jermyn Street and now assist at Cifonelli in the eighth arrondissement, but you hope to one day design your own clothes. You love old buildings, historic cities and beautiful churches, even though you're atheist. You wear hats and interesting, well-made shoes. You love dogs, but you wouldn't keep one because you think they should have the space to run free and you live in a small flat. You have many friends but only two close ones who you met when you were 18, when you went to study fashion at Central St Martins. They live in London, so you spend a lot of time on the phone or on the Eurostar. People think you are old-fashioned but you are not. You know how to do basic coding. You have the latest iPhone, and you appreciate good tech. People who don't know you very well call you 'eccentric' but they are mostly basing that on the fact that you wear a hat and have a wide vocabulary. You seem very at ease with yourself but in fact you spend a lot of time worrying about your future. You are not concerned with 'fitting in' but you are concerned with finding your place in the world and feeling settled. You are not settled yet. I don't know your age or gender, but I am pretty sure when I was 22 I would have been in love with you. Thank you for this advice and whenever I purchase maca-ron(s) I shall think of you.

Don't waste a hot second trying to fold a fitted sheet

Roll it into a ball and walk. away.

Begin every day with a song and make it a belter

It is 7.30am and just starting to get light outside. Your alarm wakes you up and you roll over and press snooze. Eight minutes later it goes off again and you press snooze again. This happens on loop for 34 minutes, as it does every morning because you are an absolute nightmare about getting up and always have been. Eventually, having reached job-threatening levels of lateness, you hit STOP on the alarm, roll out of bed, open the curtains, rub your face a bit and switch the radio on, and what do you know, it's playing one of your all-time favourite tunes. Let's say it is 'Sex Machine' by James Brown.

What happens then? Let's take it in very, very slow motion.

First, the sound from your old-timey Roberts radio manifests as waves of pressure that travel through the air of your stuffy bedroom and James Brown's counting to four enters your outer ear before hitting your eardrum. Your eardrum vibrates like, well, a drum, or like those massive speakers you see at gigs where you can actually *see* them pulsating with a dirty bass, and you're glad you clawed your way to the front of the crowd. As James Brown's brass section plays those iconic seven repeated chords, the tiny bones behind the drum do a hammering action causing a different kind of pressure and, inside your cochlea, the sound has now converted from airwaves into liquid-waves, travelling through a load of salty fluid. Sexy. These fluid movements travel though some hair cells called 'Stereocilia', which incidentally is an excellent name for a funk-soul album. This sends a signal to the auditory nerve and then onwards to the brain, which is where you interpret all these waves and hairs and fluid movements as a particular sound.

As Brown starts imploring you to 'Get Up', the auditory cortex organises the music you hear into pitch, timbre, location and duration. When the cerebellum works with the amygdala – the bit of the brain that is involved with pleasure, arousal and the release of dopamine – that's the point where you might think 'oh, it's *this* song – and it's a BELTER!' You might get a dopamine rush; this comes from your brain causing your body to start reacting in anticipation of hearing the rest of this song or even your favourite bit of the song – presumably when he references the titular *machine*. Moments prior to that favourite bit, whether it's the big rousing chorus or the emotional key change, there is activity in the part of your brain called the caudate, which is readying your body for that rush in advance. In layman's terms, your body is physically and mentally prepared for the bass to drop.

And then your body responds. Some music, and I presume 'Sex Machine' falls into this category, provokes a reaction called corticospinal excitability, which creates the urge to dance. Sometimes music can encourage blood to pump to your muscles, which is what makes your feet want to tap, and the rhythms you hear in music can cause changes in heart rate and respiratory functions and even sync up with them. And, of course, music can be hugely effective in stimulating memory – so while your brain is sending all these signals to your body, it's also causing the many neurological pathways that deal with memory to recall all the times you've heard this song, the feelings you had when you last heard it, the lyrics you associate with it and its place in your life history. (In this case, that's witnessing your husband doing an enthusiastic chair routine to this song at an old friend's very Christian wedding.)

And, in fact, all those physical responses happen instantly. Your ears, your brain, your memories, your body, can respond to a song

54

within the first second of hearing it. You feel energised, more alert, your body is moving, there is blood pumping to your muscles and in spite of the hour and the fact you are about to go to work, you find yourself smiling, even dancing.

You ARE a sex machine.

And music is a wonderful, powerful thing.

So that's what happens when you hear a belter. TLDR: it's good for you.

But what makes a belter? There are no hard and fast rules about how any given piece of music makes someone feel. Even the ones that seem obvious – Beethoven's 'Moonlight Sonata' is sad-sounding, 'Wake Up Boo' by the Boo Radleys is cheerful, Bjork's 'Hyperballad' is what outer space sounds like – these are universal feelings, surely? But, because of our memories, our cultural conditioning and the tiny, nuanced responses we've gathered to various sounds, chords, keys, instruments, types of voice or rhythms, I might hear melancholy in a song that makes you feel warm inside. I think there is a sound or a song for every situation in life and every person. Holly Willoughby, for example, is a tinkling bell, Judy Dench is an intense solo cello and Dominic Cummings is the sound of a pneumatic drill all day outside your place of work. I find it fascinating that what is ecstasy-inducing to some people is incredibly boring to others, and what makes some people feel passionate and galvanised, sounds to others like a bin falling into a hydraulic crusher or vice versa. And that upbeat, complex music can be, to some people, more calming, more centring, than silence. (A daily marital issue.)

What seem like universal responses to music, aren't as universal as we think. Take our understanding of major and minor keys; how we respond to these is as much based on cultural conditioning as an innate feeling. When I was learning about music theory growing up, the UK's very westernised system taught children that you can recognise the difference between major and minor keys or chords, because major chords sound happy and minor chords sound sad. It was only later, when I taught piano to a girl from Kazakhstan, that I realised this isn't an innate response and wouldn't be true for much of the world. She had been raised on Russian classical music, which is very largely minor, and so didn't at all associate the minor keys with sadness, but just with normality, if anything. She found it very hard to distinguish between major and minor for that reason; for her, the division was fairly arbitrary.

I've always found it hard to answer that popular question 'What music are you into?' I think people are a bit suspicious of you if you don't have an answer quickly. Many people have a band or a genre that they are passionate about – buying tickets to their gigs, getting excited about album releases (I'm showing my age here) and can confidently state 'I'm really into X' [insert Nirvana, or Mozart or ska or Mongolian Throat Singing]. I've always felt like a fraud as a musician and a music lover that I don't have that one big over-ruling passion for a group, artist or genre. My husband is a jazz nut, especially Miles Davis, and growing up one of my brothers was into the Beastie Boys and Rage Against The Machine while the other loved Eartha Kitt and Barbra Streisand. And it feels so bland, such a cheat, to answer that vital question 'What music are you into?' with 'It depends'.

But it does. I think growing up playing music and singing in many different genres made me prefer performing music to listening to a single genre. My response to some songs that I love is wanting to sing and play them myself. I want those notes under my fingers; I want those words wrapped round my teeth – I want to be in the music.

I'm a musician. I love playing music, I love learning about music and I love listening to music. Sometimes. Even as a music-lover, I have a healthy respect for silence. There's music I like and music I don't and, more importantly, there's no music at all, which I often really like. I think there are many occasions where no music is what is needed, for your brain, for your body, for the occasion. But when I do listen to music, I want it to be the right music.

So, allowing for all this nuance and individual preference, I think a 'belter' can mean something very different to different people. It probably has to pack a punch and have a certain energy, but a belter could be pop or rock or classical or musical theatre. It could be almost anything but it's probably not Nick Drake. Sorry, Nick Drake. There are different belters for different occasions, and for me, my favourite belters are ones that that've wrapped themselves around my life – through performing them or teaching them or dancing to them. There are plenty, but here are a few.

'The Way You Look Tonight' by Ella Fitzgerald

I started learning the piano when I was six. We had an old but beautiful upright in our house. It wasn't in amazing shape, but it was, crucially, *there*, and that's the reason I'm a musician. I started reaching up and having a press on the keys when I was six and my mum asked if I wanted to learn to play it, and I said yes, and that was that. Well, that wasn't that, that was the next 15 years of my life – piano lessons, piano exams, piano recitals and piano competitions.

I got into the jazz standards when I was a teenager. I had songbooks of Gershwin and Cole Porter and Irving Berlin, and I got them under my fingers, off by heart, so I could improvise around them and sing along to them by the time I left for university. 'The Way You Look Tonight', made famous by Frank Sinatra and Ella Fitzgerald, among others, was one of the first songs I learnt to sing and play off by heart. It's in C major; it's got really simple chords and beautiful lyrics.

There's something essential about the melody – it goes exactly where you want it to go. 'Some day' on G falling to C – dominant to tonic, a bare fifth, simple, complete. Then the next three phrases are a little rising sequence, get higher, closer, tone by tone upwards to the note we want – the tonic – the ringing out high C, like a bell. That then falls to the lower C, down the octave, those Cs forming words 'of you'. It's pretty perfect.

I used to have a job playing the piano in hotels and bars – you know that plinky plonky non-invasive background jazz piano that you're not quite sure if it's live or a recording? That was me. I loved such a relaxing job – one of the many jobs in music I did where the goal was in fact to blend in. It wasn't dissimilar to playing for communion in church (see below). The point was to make people feel relaxed, comfortable but not bored. I'd throw in jazz renditions of the Eastenders theme or 'Firestarter' by The Prodigy just to see if anyone noticed.

'The Way You Look Tonight' was one of the first tunes in my repertoire for this kind of work, and when I did my first jazz show at the Holywell music rooms in Oxford when I was 21 – no mic, no sound desk and no band, just me, a grand piano and the oldest concert hall in Europe – it was the first song I played. And when I performed at the Crazy Coqs in 2018, a return to performing jazz after a decade doing standup and musical comedy, it was the first song I thought of to play. I know it well but also, everyone knows it well, there's a familiarity to it that is irresistible. It's also so beautifully simple you can play it differently every time and find new ways to riff and improvise variations on it that make it a perfect song for a jazz set. It's featured in sitcoms and movies and been covered by everyone from Peggy Lee to Rod Stewart, from Maroon Five to Air. It has range, but it knows what it is at its heart. It's simple and romantic and memorable – it's just the way you want it to be.

'Dog Days Are Over' by Florence and The Machine

I think I've mentioned that I don't like exercise, especially running. Did I mention that? I'm sure I did. Running feels like a cross between having a heart attack and getting beaten up by the air, and I don't like the lies people talk about it like, 'If you start doing it regularly instead of once a year, then that overwhelming pain in your chest stops happening'. I don't believe you and I'm not willing to try it.

So, you'll understand the power that this song has when I tell you that it makes me want to *sprint*. From the very opening bars, there's an energy to it that is impossible to sit still to: somehow those guitar chords sound like a bell calling you to action. And then the hand claps come in, they let you know – something is coming . . . get ready. And then at the first chorus, you're in. They've added drums, they've got your blood pumping. Then they suddenly stop – they strip it all back, the beat drops out, it's just Florence and an acoustic guitar. Then, WHAM! Second chorus – that driving rhythm explodes into your ears, and you don't just wanna dance – you want to RUN. Fast. While flailing and punching and . . . casting spells?*

I feel this way about nearly every song on the albums *Lungs* and *Ceremonials* – these are belters without a doubt, but belters that make me feel very specifically stronger, taller and like I could probably rule the world. These aren't dance-round-your-kitchen songs, they're jump-over-a-canyon songs. And by the way, if you do ever accidentally find yourself on a treadmill, stick on 'Dog Days Are Over' on loud and let your feet take over. It's pure magic.

---

* When I feel energised and powerful, I veer towards feeling like an ethereal nature-goddess – my go-to power-persona is definitely Galadriel. There was a moment at End of the Road festival in 2013 watching St Vincent perform, while I was standing on the raised slope near the sound stage looking down at her and the crowd, and as she sang the heavens opened and this torrential rain started pouring down on us and the first thunder struck as she belted out the chorus and it all felt like some kind of magical rite.

59

'Abbot's Leigh' by Cyril Taylor

What mate? I know. If you haven't heard of Abbot's Leigh, no, it isn't the name of a folk revival band from the 70s or a popular service station on the A3. It's the name of a particular hymn tune that is an absolute belter. You might know it as the tune of 'Glorious Things Of Thee Are Spoken' but it's the melody I love, rather than those words.

I grew up going to church every week – a small Methodist church in Leicester at which my mum was the Sunday School teacher, and for which, at the age of 12, I became the organist. I was shown the ropes by the very kind old man who had been the organist for decades, Mr Jones, and when he passed away, he left me with lots of useful tips, a collection of beautiful antique sheet music and a job to do.

I think by 12 I already knew I didn't believe in God, at least not in the way the Christian Church does. But that didn't stop me from loving the music and wanting to do everything I could to make it as good as it could be. It was nerve-wracking at first; the congregation was only about 30 on a good day but you were very exposed sat up there at the front, playing not just weekly hymns but funerals, weddings, baptisms. These mattered to people, and it was important to me not just to not-cock-it-up but to make it special. To make the music for funerals sensitive but not a dirge, to choose the right music, to not be too loud but be loud enough for people to sing to and the church not to feel empty. For weddings you had to sound joyful but as you dealt with people who were often less used to singing, they needed a bit more help than the weekly congregation – I'd put the hymns in a key that made it easy for them and really try to lead them very firmly into each verse. During communion each week, I improvised music that would be peaceful but not boring.

It can take a while, communion. I did this job again in my 20s and 30s when I worked at a CofE school for eight years as a choir leader, piano teacher and resident pianist. I played in church every week and one of my major take-aways was that blessing 130 children in one sitting takes a long time and once they're blessed, they get restless. This is fairly true of adult Christians too. So, the music for communion needs to be contemplative but not monotonous – yes, it's for people to be prayerful and get lost in their own thoughts but they also want to listen and enjoy the music, so you have to get the balance right. Those 15 minutes every week, for two long stretches of my life, were really precious to me. I felt the power of what I could offer up as a musician to those listening, but also, for me, it was a tonic. It was like doing meditation; I could get lost in a trance playing that music, seeing where it led me – somewhere different every single week. It was where I felt most needed, I think, where I could be most free to create. It was where I felt the most useful.

In weekly services, I'd match up the hymn numbers with the best possible tune. I think hymns have got a bad rep – there are, inarguably, a lot of very dull hymn tunes, and too many people have experienced them played slowly and painfully in school or at church by a bored organist in a key too high to sing to and often far too slow. A lot of hymn tunes are tedious (sorry, Bach chorales) but once I found out you can match different hymn words to different tunes that still fit, I started making it a mission to always find the best possible tune to fit the words. Abbot's Leigh is a beautiful hymn tune that fits with quite a lot of hymn lyrics in the book. As a composition, it really deserves an orchestral setting and a concert hall, but even played on a lowly little electric organ it has the power to turn a hymn into something more meaningful and emotional and enjoyable, even for a heathen like me.

61

'Take Your Mama' by Scissor Sisters

As a teenager, I would put on black lipstick in my bedroom and lip sync in the mirror to Garbage songs, desperate to be as sexy and badass as Shirley Manson, and woefully disappointed that I was in fact, a blonde, well-behaved, nicely dressed A-grade student who had never had a boyfriend and who didn't entirely understand some of the explicit lyrics on Version 2.0. I loved the idea of being a rock star in a band . . . I still do actually. When I was in my third year at university, I got my first and only real taste of that. Our local nightclub, The Bridge, had a covers band on Friday nights and hired a small roster of good student singers to take turns being the lead singer each weekend. I managed to become one of them. The songs I'd sing included 'Touch Myself', 'Son Of A Preacher Man', 'Sweet Child O' Mine', 'Just the Two Of Us' and, my favourite, 'Take Your Mama' by the Scissor Sisters.

'Take Your Mama' *is* an absolute belter. Those opening chords, the beat, the tune, the up-the-octave, those lyrics – the story! Truly what we would formerly have called a CHOON. Singing it in front of a drunk, excited crowd of strangers on a Friday night in a club screaming up at me, made me feel, for the first time, like the rock star I'd always wanted to be. At that moment when Jake Shears yells 'DO IT!', I'd point the mic at the audience like I was Robbie Williams, and I'd whip my hips from side to side in time with the beats leading up to it. I loved every minute. I'd spent my school years and my music degree so far doing piano recitals, choral services, conducting, accompanying, bits of musical theatre. This felt different. I was centre stage, sweaty, sexy, loud and all the lights were on me. It was glorious.

'When I Grow Up' by Tim Minchin

Musical theatre songs make me weep convulsively. Not just the sad ones, the joyful ones sometimes do it more. It's very strange.

There's something about the sheer effort of it – the event of it. The harmonies, the blocking, the ensemble, the composition, the choreography, all coming together, live, makes it special, makes it emotional. One of the (several) reasons I probably couldn't go into musical theatre is that when I perform songs at home at the piano, I start crying halfway through. You'd think it would be a useful dramatic tool but no, if you actually start bawling, your throat closes up and your voice just stops mid-note. I appeared in a production of *The Last Five Years*, a very emotional two-hander musical by Jason Robert Brown in 2007, and every night I struggled to get through 'I'm Still Hurting' – the very beautiful, very moving opening number – without actually breaking down and crying. And it's too late to explain to a reviewer: 'No, well, yes, my voice did break but only through how much I was *feeling it*.'

They all get me weeping: 'No One Is Alone' from *Into The Woods*, Sara Bareilles' 'She Used To Be Mine', 'You Will Be Found' from *Dear Evan Hansen*, 'Me and The Sky' from *Come From Away* and just anything by William Finn . . . I mean actually hundreds of songs; I just break. I've seen some shonky musicals in my time, but there's usually at least one moment, even in the worst musical, that makes you feel something.

Matilda doesn't fall into the inexplicably moving musicals – it's totally explicable – it's brilliant. Tim Minchin wrote the songs. He's one of my comedy heroes (I only have two – him and Victoria Wood); I first saw him perform live at the Edinburgh Fringe in 2006 and it was a game changer. He was a phenomenal musician – an accomplished, fast-fingered jazz pianist, singer, a talented poet and comic – but what threw me for a loop was that with no apology, he included sad or dramatic songs in his show. A revelation for me – just taking tentative steps into solo comedy: the idea that not every second in an hour-long show has to be funny. When he sang 'White Wine In The Sun', a slow ballad about missing Christmas and his family in Australia, the audience was in tears . . . in a comedy show! In fact, it seemed like they loved him more for it! This was the revelation I'd always looked for. I had found people enjoyed my comedy songs but I wanted to do more – I had a backlog of emotional songs and poems that weren't funny that I still wanted to perform. I wanted to do shows that were funny AND a bit sad. Did this mean I was allowed? It seemed so.

In the years after this I went about writing and gigging my first solo show for the Edinburgh Fringe (which would be largely funny but with a real emotional thread and a tearjerker song towards the end), while Minchin got bigger and bigger – arena tours, orchestras and then writing internationally acclaimed musicals. And *Matilda* was exactly what you'd hope from him – clever, articulate, irreverent and at times heartbreaking.

I ran the children's choir I mentioned earlier with my friend Amy for eight years in a primary school – she did the leading and conducting, I did the accompanying and arranging. Together, we taught them this song, which we both loved, for a competition. Hearing them sing it – a bit nervous, untrained, natural, not musical theatre kids with perfect pitch – was even more emotional than hearing it in the West End. Songs, after all, are for enjoying, not perfecting, and not competing . . . [Sidebar: they won.]

'When I Grow Up' features children swinging on swings, singing about what they'll do when they grow up; how they'll be stronger and taller and cleverer and brave enough to fight the monsters under the bed in order to be a grown up. It makes you think of the child you were, the children you know, and all the things we didn't know back then about being a grown up. It makes you cry for yourself, and for them: for all the things you don't want kids to have to find out, but they will, for all the things you didn't know you'd find out, but you have. You want them to keep thinking that being a grown up is all about getting to have the treats their mum won't let them have.

On the other hand, it's heartbreaking because they're right – being a grown up *is* about trying to be brave and strong. And, yes, you can have a Twix for breakfast, if you want to.

'I'm A Believer' by The Monkees

This was the 'hymn' we got everyone to sing together at our wedding. An everyone-join-in, top-of-your-voice, more-shouting-than-singing belter. It is an anthem of joy and surprise and revelation.

'I thought love was only true in fairytales.'

This wasn't quite my feeling when I met my husband. By the time I met him, I was already a romantic; I already believed that love was real; I'd been in love before, and so had he. But this felt different. When we got together, it was love, yes, and more; it was a love that feels instantly like you've found your life in someone. And I had. I thought that was only true in fairytales.

'Tightrope' by Janelle Monáe

Let's be clear – Janelle Monáe is a goddess and I love her and so does everyone else. She's sexy and fierce and smart and queer and she wore trousers that look like a massive vagina and that's all I want in an icon.

When lockdown struck in 2020, my husband and I would lip sync along with our favourite songs at each other to pass the time and we ended up recording some just for fun and putting them on Twitter. We called it #lockdownlipsync. We started doing them daily and, with so much time on our hands, the production values ramped up day by day until we were using disco lights and a smoke machine. My favourite to lip sync to was 'Tightrope'; the song is a joy to get your lips around and practically medicinal at a time when you can't leave the house and you urgently need some funk, some rap and a killer brass section.

I think singing in a choir, whether you're a good singer or a rusty pipe, is one of the best things a person can do. Choral singing isn't just about you making music, it's about joining in with others, making a commitment, listening carefully, learning something new, being confident but also blending in.

I've been in various choirs since I was at primary school – some amateur some professional, swinging between alto, soprano and conductor – so yes, I'm biased. I'm a lifelong fan. I'm a choir nut. I've got a harmony hard-on. I crave the stave.

I've had some amazing experiences in choirs. I've performed renaissance polyphony at Lambeth Palace for the Archbishop of Canterbury, Handel's 'Messiah' at Blenheim Palace at Christmas and belted out Britten's 'War Requiem' in a mass choir in Poland. I've sung in choirs for weddings, funerals and bat mitzvahs and have performed everything from Parry's anthem 'I Was Glad' to Shania Twain's 'From This Moment On'. I've sung in English, French, Italian, Polish, German, Yiddish, Swahili, Latin and fake Latin on the soundtrack to the video game *Killzone 2*. Sometimes you're in a choir for years and sometimes for a few hours, brought together just to sing for a particular event, but it is always bonding. There's always a feeling that you created something special for that moment, even if that moment is the soundtrack to *Killzone 2*.

Sometimes singing in a choir feels peaceful and serene and intimate. Sometimes it feels like a wrecking ball. But a really good wrecking ball – like the wrecking ball from the song 'Wrecking Ball'. One of the pieces that feels like this is 'I Was Glad' by Parry. If you don't know it, look it up and listen to the version with orchestral accompaniment, not organ (I'm not a huge fan of the organ, especially for a former organist). It is a true belter. It's so powerful and grand, it's usually reserved for coronations in cathedrals and abbeys with vast choirs and acoustics to stretch the sound up to the sky, but I've sung it in a small chapel, with a choir of 10, and it was majestic as hell.

'Walk of Life' by Dire Straits

'Walk of Life' has a special place in our household. I think we all know it's a bit cheesy, but it's a family belter, no question. Quite soon into our relationship, my husband and I started doing a simple dance to it which we've come to call the elbow dance. It's not hard, and you'd recognise it – elbows bent and lift them up alternately on the beat. Like a more co-ordinated birdie dance, with the 'Walk of Life', you start slowly and then go double time when the drums kick in.

When lockdown happened in 2020, we started doing a weekly online gig over Zoom called Tuesday Night Club. We started doing it around the same time as the online #lockdownlipsync and we'd end every show with a lip sync battle. But we'd begin every show with us dancing inanely to a belter, and that first week we elbow-danced to 'Walk of Life'. We looked mad but luckily everyone in the audience felt mad by that point, and it seemed to capture a mood. Across 2020 and 2021, we did the elbow dance at the start of each gig to a different tune every week, for a year. By the end of it, we watched as hundreds of viewers on Zoom joined in with us – it became our signature move, like MC Hammer's, and equally as culturally important.

My step-kids started joining in with the elbow dance when 'Walk of Life' would come on in the car and we'd roll down the M40 doing synchronised elbows. It is an act of love and ridiculousness. It makes me very happy that two teenagers with all their own stuff going on can go all-in on something so absolutely absurd. It says a lot when a tune is so banging it can inspire your Gen Z kids to look so deeply uncool for a few minutes and dance with their dad.

The first thing I want to teach my child is how to do the elbow dance so that we can operate as a five-person unit, travelling down the motorway, Dire Straits ringing out of the windows, all of us synchronising our elbows in unashamed and unmitigated celebration of the power of The Belter.

So, yes, start your day with a song. Make it a belter, whatever a belter is to you. Whether you start your day with a shimmy or a mosh, with funk or punk, R&B or G&S, an aria or Ariana. Whether you sing along, lip sync along, dance along or just stand still and naked at your window taking it all in, find your tune, turn it up and make your day a belter.

Never trust a man with only one eyebrow

Pretty sure this is ableist.

Stay at home and everything will be okay

I started writing this chapter at the very start of 2021, AKA 'Lockdown 3', AKA 'Lockdown 2' because we don't know if that blip in November really counted as a *legit* lockdown, AKA Dry Dry Dry January, AKA The Christmas Payback, AKA When Will This End, AKA Definitely Not By February When Boris Said It Would, AKA The Lockdown That We Should Have Done In Autumn, AKA Hubris 2.0.

I really enjoy the fact that this piece of advice was written:

a)   On the back of a Royal Mail note I presume they found in their bag, and

b)   On 28th March 2018, at a time when the writer would have no way of imagining that it would become the most valuable piece of advice in the world; that this advice would become a life-or-death matter.

I remember first hearing about the virus in January 2020. My husband mentioned it to me quite a few times; he was reading any news articles he could find about it and was quite worried. I remember he said, 'I think this could get really bad.' I thought he was being dramatic and over-the-top and didn't worry much at all. It turns out I was very wrong and he was very right and I'm sure that, if it weren't for the worldwide death toll, incumbent recession and ongoing threat to life as we know it, he would chalk it up as an incredibly satisfying marital victory.

There were news stories about it through February but never headline news, and life carried on. Bit by bit things started to get cancelled, based on people's individual decisions (as opposed to government advice). In early March, myself and comedian Ellie Taylor were booked to host the Stylist Awards. We were very excited – Ellie and I both love the chance to get glammed up, and it was our first job co-hosting together, which made it double the fun. It was an international event with women from all over the world flying in to attend. We'd had rehearsals, meetings, chosen dresses, had fittings and had written our script for it – we hoped to be pale imitations of Tina Fey and Amy Poehler, in my case, very pale. It was a huge undertaking.

It was suddenly cancelled 24 hours before the event. I was very slow to catch on to the direction things were going in, and I can tell that because both me and Ellie were very shocked about that first big cancellation. I think I used the word 'overkill', little knowing that that was exactly what the organisers were avoiding. I had no idea at the time how important cancellations like that were. International guests, all coming over here and mixing, it would have been disastrous. We could have killed off Margaret Atwood!

By mid-March, things were still left up to the public to decide. Theatres, cinemas, bars, restaurants, gyms were all open. All warnings were advisory – *try* not to go the pub, *please* wash your hands, work from home if it is *possible*, *probably* don't go abroad *if* you can help it. It put a huge amount of responsibility on the public to do the right thing. And we didn't really yet know what the right thing was.

On 17 March 2020, I was at the Fortune Theatre in the West End preparing to perform in *Austentatious*, my improvised comedy show. No major theatres had cancelled shows at this point so, following discussions between us and the producers and the theatre, we went ahead with getting ready for the show. We arrived and got into our costumes, curled our hair, put on our makeup, performed our cult-like pre-show warm-up rituals etc. It did all feel eerie. Everything did by now – we were all living in uncertainty before that first lockdown. The audience had been let in and were waiting in the foyer. Doors were set to open at 7.15pm.

At 6.45pm, the manager of the theatre came backstage and told us that discussions were happening between all London theatres and that they were considering closing the shows imminently. We were told to wait for more information. Ten minutes later, the manager returned and said tonight's show would be cancelled immediately and all shows for the foreseeable future, both here, across the West End and all major theatres across the country were all closing simultaneously at 7pm. Our audience and audiences across the country were told to leave the theatre, to go home, that refunds would be issued. We returned to our dressing room, got out of costume, back into jeans and trainers and left the theatre just as thousands of performers and audience members were leaving theatres all over central London. There were crowds of us all head-ing to the tubes. It was oddly quiet; I think we were digesting what just happened and what it would mean. The drama of this happen-ing to so many, at the exact same time and us all taking that same journey home, was a pretty stark moment of realisation – this was the start of the really big stuff.

It was only the day after all theatres had, themselves, taken the decision to close their doors that the government issued the order for them to close, on 18th March. In so much of this, people acted first, and the government followed.

The official UK lockdown began on 23rd March 2020.

That first wave felt very different to later lockdowns. By our third go round, we knew what lockdown was – that what was in store was bleak and hard with no clear end-date in sight. That first wave, starting in March 2020, held something else. It was bad, certainly. But there was a sense of excitement; no-one had lived through anything like this. We were shut in our houses, schools shut, work closed, no cafes, no pubs, no shops except essentials. You weren't allowed to travel in your car unless it was an essential journey. It was awful but it was so incredibly weird that the awfulness was a little mitigated by the sheer novelty of it all. What was going to happen? What would this feel like? How long would it last? Would we all start wearing grey linen uniforms like in a dystopian novel? Would we genuinely run out of toilet paper and what would we use then? Leaves!? The weekly clapping for the NHS – how long would that last? Forever? Will we now be part of a neighbourly community for the rest of time? Will we start singing songs in the streets and sharing firewood? There were lots of war comparisons, but of course, it wasn't quite like a war. It had the death toll, the fear of the unknown, the restricted movements and, initially, panic-buying. It also had a feeling that we were all in this together. We weren't really – some were 'in it' in their second home, a three acre estate in Gloucestershire, and some were 'in it' on minimum wage in a 15th storey bedsit and some were 'in it' in Barnard Castle. We weren't all in the same situation, but there was a sense of camaraderie, a shared strangeness and wonder at something that was totally new to all of us.

Of course, the novelty wore off quite quickly. Once we realised this wasn't for a few weeks, but months, it really was depressing. And then we got to the end of *The Queens Gambit* on Netflix and things got really bad. March 2020 to March 2021 was an incredibly emotionally draining time, not just because of the lockdowns and the disease but because the country as a whole was given warnings, rules, then hope, then release, then false hope, then warnings, then terrible news, then relief. You have to stop work! Stay out of school! You can go back to work! You can go out to eat! You SHOULD go out to eat! GET BACK IN THE HOUSE! But DO go to school! Don't go to work though! NOW DON'T GO TO SCHOOL! This will be over in three weeks. You can see your family at Christmas! YOU CAN'T SEE YOUR FAMILY AT CHRISTMAS! GET IN THE HOUSE! But go back to schoo—DON'T go to school. It was mentally exhausting and confusing and the only release from it all was to communally scream 'Covidiots' at people on beaches and buy a new fabric mask, while wishing we were on that beach.

If you cast your mind back, we knew so little about Covid-19 at the start. We didn't know how catching it was beyond 'very'. They didn't know how it was transmitted – through touch, or droplets or breathing or sending bad vibes. They didn't know all the symptoms. They didn't know how long it lasted – we still don't. They didn't know that masks were useful.

My husband and I got Covid very early – in March 2020. Our symptoms only matched with some of the official ones. We had no cough. We only briefly had a fever. Our main symptoms were severe muscle ache and fatigue. It was like flu. Proper flu, not a bad cold. Proper flu where you have to say to people 'no, not, like, coldey flu – ACTUAL flu – like InfluENZA'. To let them know just how much you're suffering. My husband Marcus had it worse than me – worse aches, worse dizziness, and it lasted about a week longer. And then just as we were both recovering, we both one day suddenly lost our senses of taste and smell. Totally. It was surreal. We were sticking our heads in coffee bags or over garlic to test it out, and we got nothing. Zilch. So weird. Bearing in mind we'd been ill for a couple of weeks and also lost our sense of smell, you can probably imagine the horrors of the day when we both started getting our sense of smell back and realised just how much each of us stank. My God. Emergency Bath Day in the Brigstocke household.

Our work evaporated. I had a thirty-date Spring tour booked, which was obviously postponed until Autumn, then postponed again till 2021, and again till 2022. All TV appearances were cancelled. Live gigs cancelled. Our income disappeared very suddenly, which was scary. We couldn't get any compensation from Rishi Sunak's schemes as we were part of the three million who fell between the gaps. But we were the lucky ones compared to many friends. If it'd happened three years earlier, I'd have had no savings and wouldn't have been able to pay the rent. As it was, I'd just had a couple of good years so had some savings to fall back on and fall back on them I *have*. I've fallen on my savings very hard and with little warning. In the trust building exercise of my career, I am very tall Ken from HR, blindly falling backwards heavily into the trembling arms of tiny Sue from Purchasing AKA my savings account, petite, fragile and yet to recover.

It was a bad time. A bad time for everyone. We all had some burdens in common:

financial disaster
fear of illness or death
boredom
Joe Wicks
yeast shortages
home-schooling
isolation
being the first on your street to stop clapping
running out of films
childcare
tensions between friends and family
Gavin Williamson

But, as in normal life, we all had individual burdens too. For me and my husband, with identi-careers, both of us simultaneously had no work. After a few months, once online gigs got going and the odd outside gig in summer, we were getting about 10% of our regular income to keep the household going. This financial fear and loss of career coincided with losing our first baby – weeks in hospital and then recuperating, physically and emotionally. Then the remaining lockdown woes, which everyone was going through. But, amongst all that stress, trauma and worry were good things. There nearly always is some good in a dark situation. I'd like to dedicate the rest of the chapter to that. Here's some things I learnt from lockdown that I hope to carry forward with me in life.

Get on Board with Board Games

One of the major complaints people have about board games is that they're too long or too complicated. Well, picture the scene: It's lockdown 2021. You're trapped indoors with a partner or your family with nothing else to do. You've already exhausted both the 'Cheerful British sitcoms' and 'True Crime Documentaries' categories on Netflix. You're sick of making bread. The online 'school day' ended unexpectedly at 1.30pm because there was a glitch on Teams. That very long, very complicated game starts to seem a little bit more appealing, doesn't it?

Now, you can start off with your Monopolys and your Risks. We know the rules, the games take ages, there'll be a fall out, but we all know where we stand. But fall-outs in a trapped household aren't ideal, so you can limit this by ensuring no one player has a huge advantage. If someone in your bubble is a hedge fund manager, don't let them be the banker in Monopoly. Don't play Operation with a heart surgeon – it's an unfair advantage. I imagine that advantage might cross over into Jenga too – professionally steady hands is cheating. Talking of cheating, avoid playing a 1989 edition of Trivial Pursuit with your 12-year-old. You may know what year Duncan Goodhew won Olympic Gold, but you shouldn't wield that over your children on a self-adulating trivia power trip.

Speaking of which, beware the Rage-Quit. Of course, there will be tension but the goal is to avoid any household member:

flipping the board
swiping the pieces to the side
'accidentally' throwing carbonated sugary drink over the game
storming upstairs
storming to the sofa
passive-aggressively saying 'forget it, I'll just watch'
setting fire to the rules pamphlet.

Remember: the aim is to make the house a happier place. And to win, obviously – there's no participation certificates here, snowflakes! Haha! Another double six! Suck it!

Sorry. Do not behave like that.

So, while lockdown forced us into exploring board games in a way we might not have considered, it turns out they are really fun, EVEN outside of a burgeoning international crisis. A board game is for life, not just for Christmas-when-you-are-suddenly-forbidden-from-leaving-the-house-depending-on-your-tier.

Some games provide more than just fun. Balderdash, for example, involves making up meanings and definitions and trying to pass them off as real. Inventive and fun and great for teaching your children how to lie! Coup and Risk are great for a getting in practice for when the revolution comes and we have to run a new system of government. Dixit is a whimsical game of beautifully painted picture cards that could easily double as artwork for your wall. And Ker Plunk has a very long set up time – ideal. And a guaranteed level playing field. Unless one of you is a heart surgeon (see earlier).

Walk the Line

To be fair, I've always loved walking. Long-walking. Long, steady walking. When I was growing up, 'going on walks' was a major leisure activity – around the Leicester countryside at weekends, and our holidays were in the Lake District, hiking and climbing. The years I lived in Oxford were big walking years; I didn't have a bike, so I was walking miles around the city from lecture to lecture when I studied there or from job to job when I worked there. Even living in London, as a non-driver, and working in places from Southall to Mudchute, from Kensington to New Cross; walking has been a necessity and a pleasure. I'm basically a hobbit without the entourage. Similar feet though.

The best available option for getting outside during lockdown was going for a walk. Gyms were all closed, which affected my weekly gym routine in no way at all. Most places of exercise were closed: climbing walls, swimming pools, crazy golf (best kind of exercise). You were allowed outside once a day to exercise so you better make it good. Running was an option obviously, but a terrible one that I hate. And you weren't allowed to drive to any local beauty spots unless you needed to test your eyesight in the company of your wife and toddler on her birthday. So, I walked.

Every day, my husband and I would walk out our front door and meander through our local urban streets finding new roads we hadn't been down, new turns, new paths, and we'd just keep going for hours. In summer this was an easy choice. In winter it was more of a challenge. It felt like a very British mentality to freely choose to go out for a long walk in wet snow in mid-February and to DECIDE to ENJOY IT.

But now 'going for walks' as often as life allows is a fixture. Even if there's not much green space around your area, you learn to appreciate the streets, the town, the skyscrapers or shop fronts or back alleys and all the different buildings you find. My favourite thing to appreciate was the details of other people's houses.

DO

Appreciate other people's houses as you walk. A bay window, brightly coloured door or even unexpected turret (on a terrace!) can be a delight.

DON'T

Let your porch porn habit spill over into illegal surveillance. If you must shout 'PHWOAR look at the feature wall on THAT' or 'GET IN! I can see RIGHT IN to their basement' then at least do it from the other side of the road, not (as we did) directly outside their front door.

Get Your Gladrags On

Many of us will have spent lockdown in the classic Covid uniform of baggy jogging bottoms, grey sweaters, novelty socks and that T-shirt you might've actually worn in bed all last week, but it doesn't smell yet so it's probably fine. Even if we had important, formal meetings on Zoom, we quickly realised that colleagues could only see us from the collarbone up. If you threw any blouse over whatever you were wearing and put on any bright lipstick, you were sorted. Even when the rest of your face is haggard, your hair's matted and you're wearing a faded T-shirt you got free at Frankie & Benny's, a 'strong lip' as the professionals say, can transform you instantly from 'sickly stray' to 'hipster glam'. I'd recommend bright orange lippy for that purpose – it screams 'I am capable of making strong decisions' and I do mean *screams*.

But what started becoming clear was that it was worth putting on some more interesting clothes to stop us going crazy at the tedium of our own self-image. All those years women spent saying we were putting a dress on 'for ourselves, not for men'? Well, lockdown proved that 100% true. Life usually gives you a reason to experiment with your image; whether it's curl your hair for a dinner party, put on some nice new jeans to go on a date, or buy some of those metallic chunky brogues you see K-Pop singers wearing and you have a (false) notion you could pull off. Well, when life gives you no reason to make an effort, you have to do it for *no* reason. Or, rather, because it makes you feel better, it brightens your space for you and your household and it's another place to put your creativity.

It's not about looking sexy. But that can be nice, too! Making yourself feel attractive during a year where your vibe veers between 'cosy' and 'grubby sloth' can be a challenge, so in order to remember sometimes that you *are* hot, give yourself a visual reminder. I recommend taking a selfie to preserve the moment. One person's narcissism is another's self-love. And sexy is different for different people. For some it might be wearing matching underwear under whatever you're wearing on top or putting some Brylcreem in your hair, for others it might be luminescent leggings or a shirt that shows off your guns.

But it's not just feeling attractive, but feeling special, unusual, individual, unique. It helped in lockdown and it's fun in normal life, too. Do clothes swaps with friends; get some new swag for free. Surprise yourself. Look at the bottom of the cupboards at the clothes you haven't worn for ages and wear them (unless they're a gilet). Wear things you'd never put together. On days when you're feeling a bit grey, find the sequin top you wore for your sister's hen do or the novelty tie your daughter bought you for a joke. To put it simply, on some days, pro-actively *choose* something you want to wear, not something you *might as well* wear. Whatever makes you feel shiny.*

Stand By Your Fad

The phrase 'it's just a fad' is often a negative one, whether it's meant to comfort or to criticise.

'My son's gone and got frosted tips.'
'Don't worry I'm sure it's just a fad.'

'Mark's made a focaccia every week this month!'
'That's nice, it's probably just a fad though.'

A 'fad' is used to dismiss someone's activities on the basis that they won't last forever. But does that matter? Just because something doesn't last forever it doesn't mean it isn't worthwhile.†

Which brings me to sourdough. Much was made of the middle-class penchant for men suddenly getting an interest in making fancy bread over lockdown. (Yes, my husband was one of them.) It wasn't the only craft that had a sudden uptake from bored or frazzled people looking to fill their time or destress. CNN reported that across the world, people were discovering crafts and hobbies during this period that they'd never had time for in normal life.[10] From model train sets to dressmaking, origami or sketching, people found comfort and creativity in new ways. And it can only be a good thing. I took up embroidery for a few weeks – ordered the frames and some thread and started off freehand, in something that resembled flowers, fancying myself as a bit of a historical lady. I

---

* See page 243.
† I've always had the same attitude about relationships. Unless it was toxic or damaging, I've never agreed with people that the end of a relationship means it was, by default, an unsuccessful one. My two previous long-term relationships ended after a few years because they had run their course but we had a great time while they lasted and I think they were successful relationships. They just didn't last forever. You can stay in an unhappy marriage until you die (please don't!) that doesn't make it a successful relationship.

stopped after a few weeks. I think at some point I'll go back to it, but even if not, it was a fun new thing to try, and I created something. Lockdown gave us time to discover new things and even time to abandon them. But it doesn't invalidate them. If your husband made fresh bread for a couple of months and then stopped, then why not fondly remember the period when your husband made fresh bread for a couple of months. If you got obsessed with crocheting and made a very misshapen hat before quitting forever, then congrats on your hat. Congrhats.

Hobbies and interests will come and go, but I think it's worth being grateful for them anyway. And if lockdown gave us the time to try out things we never would have before then thank you to lockdown and I hope that in the years to come, we remember to keep on discovering, obsessing over, then quitting, many more brilliantly pointless activities.

Embrace Square Eyes

I have never so much appreciated the television as in 2020/21. The number one goal for television changed – no longer was I quite as enticed by one-off high-quality dramas. The gold standard of lockdown viewing was very long-running highly addictive programming that, ideally, everyone else was also watching. You wanted something that provided the comfort of returning to it, that you could talk to friends about and share opinions and outrage, and most importantly that filled a lot of time.

British people spent 40% of their waking hours watching TV during the height of the coronavirus pandemic and we doubled our time spent watching subscription services like Netflix.[11] Across all platforms, programmes like *Tiger King, Selling Sunset, Married At First Sight, Cobra Kai, Normal People, The Queens Gambit* and *Strictly Come Dancing* became touchstones for us to connect with others over. It didn't matter if we loved them or hated them; the point was that we had watched them together, albeit in different houses, and had a shared experience we could talk about. Who would have thought Bill Bailey doing the American Smooth could become such an important cultural touchstone?

There was another curious phenomenon to emerge from 2020 on our screens. Perhaps due to us living in a dual state of high-stakes-fear for our lives and also mundane everyday boredom, television divided itself very largely into two categories – murder or craft. We were offered serial killer documentaries like *The Staircase*, *The Confessions Killer*, *Night Stalker*, the *Ted Bundy tapes*, *Don't Fuck With Cats*, as well as serial killer dramas like *Des*, *You*, *The Serpent* and *Mindhunter*.

We simultaneously got invested in craft and skill programmes like *The Great Pottery Throwdown*, *The Repair Shop*, *Portrait Artist of the Year*, *Blown Away* (about glass-blowing), *Interior Design Masters*, *Junior Bake-Off*, *The Great British Sewing Bee*, *Glow-Up* (about make-up artistry), *The Big Flower Fight* and *The Chop*, a show about woodwork that got pulled after one episode because one of the contestants had Nazi symbols tattooed on his face.[12] Just goes to show, craft really is for all types of people.

When I was growing up watching too much television was a vice – 'it'll turn your eyes square'. Anything that your parents didn't grow up with as routine is often then portrayed by them as a modern plague that should be rationed. In the late 18th to 19th century, reading 'novels' (a fairly recent invention) was seen as a petty, pointless activity of little worth – the Regency equivalent of reality television – fluff that wasn't good for the mind.

When I was growing up, reading a novel was definitely a cultural activity to be encouraged whereas television was never that. We watched it, of course, but like everyone else I knew, we grew up knowing you could watch 'too much'. Now, in our household, watching a film together as a family is THE wholesome activity and the modern plague is the kids on their phones watching endless YouTube clips and muttering things to each other on Snapchat.

Video games have, in some circumstances, made the transition from mind-numbing social threat to a nourishing family activity. Not if you're playing *Red Dead Redemption* with your toddlers – that wouldn't be as nourishing, and they wouldn't do very well.

What will come along when Generation Z are the parents? By then, perhaps YouTube videos and exchanging words with friends over Snapchat will be the valued, wholesome activity and perhaps they will worry about their children . . . watching holograms of celebrities, sitting next to them on the sofa or spending too much time in their VR headsets.

'Get your head out of that book.'

'Switch the telly off.'

'Put your phone down.'

'Turn off that hologram.'

There will always be technologies we feel we have to moderate, but lockdown gave us all a real reliance on and appreciation of good entertainment. It's not a dubious indulgence lurking to corrupt the minds of the young but something that can bring us together, comfort us when we're alone and give us something to talk about with distant friends when it is so hard to share other experiences. I've never felt more grateful for every drama, film, documentary or incredibly vacuous and morally compromising reality TV show.

Get a House Plant

If you're spending 24 hours a day in your house, it really helps to have something in it that is fresh and natural and alive and growing that you can tend to. I'm aware children and pets can provide those things but I'm not going to recommend you get a pet or have a child – that level of advice is a tad too life-altering for me to dole out in a book, and after all, I'd feel like it was false advertising to describe most pets, or children, as 'fresh'.

Though it felt more important in lockdown, I'm now a big fan of plants in the house even though I have an appalling record with them. Between us, my husband and I have killed enough plants in a year to create a special feature garden at Kew called 'Afterlife: The Realm of the Undead Hosta'. The problem is we don't have an agreed watering system. Two possible dangers occur: either, we both assume the other one has done the watering and so no-one does it and the plants die from thirst (farewell Michael the Money Plant), or we both step up and do the watering at separate times, and the plants get watered twice and drown (RIP, Billy The Orchid). We've managed to kill a cactus, unbelievably from under-watering. I feel a bit cross about that one. I think the advertising campaign for cacti is misleading: surely they're sold on the pretext of needing absolutely no watering at all, but it turns out they do need 'some' and apparently it now suddenly isn't okay to ignore a cactus for six months to a year. Very unfair.

On the other hand, there are two plants we love because they've survived against the odds in what a horticulturalist would probably call a 'hostile environment' i.e. our house. Lazarus, so called because he's lived in the corner of our living room for years and the whole family thought he was dead. He was doing no harm, just a twiggy spectacle in a nice pot, so we left him. Then a year ago, on a bit of a whim, I watered him and the very next day a green leaf had sprouted! He had risen, he had risen indeed! We watered him more and over a few months, he's now leafy and lush and definitely alive. From a dead twig! And we've got a palm in our bedroom that is just brilliantly undemanding and seems to be getting more beautiful as time passes – we call her Jane Fronda.

So, as time goes on, even now that we are allowed out of the house, I'd recommend house plants for anyone. They take up less space than a pet, need less attention than a child and have fewer opinions than a life partner. You'll always win an argument with a fern.

Water Your Friends

Just as it's easy to forget to water plants until they're a dry husk and it's too late, it is easy to forget to keep topping up friendships that you think of as just being there indefinitely. Friendships need a bit of care and attention, even when lives are busy and strange and getting back to normal.

For me, lockdown definitely brought me closer to friends, even though we weren't allowed to meet. We all needed each other more than ever. For many friends, lockdown coincided with other big life events. Several lost mothers and fathers, some had to move back home to look after a vulnerable parent. Some were struggling to conceive, others were coping with newborns. Some re-evaluated their relationships – getting engaged or breaking up. Some had breakdowns or became depressed. Many had to totally rethink their careers. Not all of this was caused by Covid; much of it wasn't. But life carries on, and while lockdown was the universal problem in everyone's lives, it wasn't the biggest or only problem in everyone's lives. And I felt so lucky to have friends to lean on, heavily at times. We could rarely meet. But we talked and WhatsApped and Zoomed and chatted and had deep-and-meaningfuls as well as stupid-and-pointlesses.

But inevitably as time moves on and life starts to become normal, we will take each other for granted again. We'll probably be less in touch even though it will be easier to meet. It's in keeping with that very human habit we all have of, when something is more readily available, you take less of it. During lockdown, friends were the last chocolate bar in the house that you'd hidden and saved and that you have cravings for. In normal life they can become a bar of chocolate in a chocolate factory; a factory that you own and you can have whenever you want; you've got a massive flume of chocolate for god's sake – why would you remember to value it? But I hope I don't forget how much we all need each other and how much of a lifeline they were. I hope I keep my friendships watered and fed and fresh and don't treat them like Lazarus the houseplant – they deserve more than occasional attention. Just to really wear out the analogy – plants don't thrive from being ignored and then getting a huge bucket of water thrown on them suddenly. They need a little bit, all the time, to stay healthy. That was my advice to myself after lockdown. Don't wait for a pandemic, a drama, a loss or a big life event to pull you all together. Keep your friends watered, regularly, because you need them more than you know.

I have wondered what inspired this piece of advice. 'Stay at home and everything will be okay' could be the warning of an agoraphobe or an introvert. It could be a veiled threat: a way of telling me to stop doing shows, or else! It could be someone gleefully revelling in JOMO – the joy of missing out.

The year 2020 proved this advice to be untrue – while staying at home was necessary, it didn't solve everything. Not everyone was okay staying at home. People suffered with loneliness and depression. Children missed out on education. Parents were overworked with no childcare. Livelihoods were lost because of it. People in abusive relationships were trapped in terrible situations. It was not okay for everyone.

'Stay at home and everything will be okay' suggests that staying at home will make everything okay – this is obviously not true. But if you separate this advice out, it holds a certain truth, one we were clinging to during lockdown; that *in spite* of staying at home, things might be alright.

'Stay at home'
  and
'Everything will be okay'

This could have been the national message rolled out to us. There is reassurance there. Everything has not *been okay* while we stayed at home. But perhaps, now, it will be.

What's for you won't pass you

This chapter is about miscarriage and baby loss. If you have experience of this, and if you are triggered by these topics then please cut yourself some slack and skip a chapter. Don't push yourself too hard – you don't owe any-one the favour of hearing their story when you're dealing with your own.

3rd October 2020

I got pregnant in Spring 2020 – during that first proper, life-chang-ing lockdown at the start of the Covid-19 pandemic. It wasn't anything to do with lockdown, though. It wasn't conceived in a spirit of panic or boredom or 'Why not, there's literally nothing else to do'. For us it was very planned and hoped for; we'd been trying for a while, and it just happened to happen then, and I was so excited. It was my first. I was about to turn 36.

When I was 18 weeks pregnant, I had some bleeding and I called up the maternity unit as you're advised to, and they said I should come to the hospital straight away. I felt fairly complacent about it – I've got what my husband and I have darkly termed 'a bleedy cervix' (this got a mixed reaction from the midwives, quite a tough crowd) – I do just bleed a bit in general and had already bled a little earlier in the preg-nancy, on and off. So, I was surprised when the doctor told me I had to stay in hospital; they were worried. And now so was I. It wasn't a 'normal amount' of bleeding.

Anyone who's been pregnant will know the absolute mindfuck-ery of deciphering what is a 'normal' amount of bleeding and what's not. Spotting is usually fine. Bleeding is *sometimes* fine but sometimes really not fine. The difference between 'spotting' and 'bleeding' is often very hard to judge – what if it's neither a tiny drip nor enough to fill a pad – but the difference in result is vast and has overwhelming consequences. If you have spotting, that's totally normal, just carry on as normal. If you have bleeding, that's very worrying – go to A&E immediately. You may have a medium amount of blood, but there's no medium response available between those two things – cue me endlessly re-googling the definition of 'spotting', image searching pictures of women's pants to see what 'light bleeding' looks like, constantly trying to find more accurate parameters and staring at a teaspoon trying to work out whether the amount of blood that went into the toilet just now was less than that (absolutely fine) or more than that (panic stations).

I was admitted to the ward and monitored – and got sufficiently scared. I flipped 180 from complacency to the, actually quite fair, assumption that I might be in the early stages of miscarrying. And no-one can say 'no, don't worry; you're not miscarrying' because you might be or you might do in a couple of days or weeks, and they have to allow for that. So, monitoring was key. I was suddenly paying incredibly close attention to what emerged from my vagina. And so was everyone else. I got used to midwives and doctors coming in and just asking to view the sanitary pad I was wearing – I'd whip my pants down and they'd stare at the red stain, with high curiosity, mild surprise, and, later on, occasional pleasure, like it was a bold new artwork by Damian Hurst. The policy from the start was they'd keep me in until I stopped bleeding for a full 24 hours. Whatever was going on, they were honest enough to say, there was nothing they could really do about it, except monitor, try to keep me safe and keep staring at my sanitary towels.

After a week, the bleeding went down, and I was allowed to go home. They thought it might have been a low-lying placenta, which had now righted itself. At home, for the next 10 days, I fell surprisingly quickly back into confidence in the pregnancy – even messaging people who had offered us a pram and talking about the year to come as if all was now well. I thought it was, we had now experienced the scary bump in the road that you fear, and it was over.

Then the bleeding started again, but this time with sharp pains, for days, which I found out later had been early contractions. I went in for my 20-week scan and there were several problems – the pain, the bleeding, a shortened cervix . . .

I was admitted to hospital again. I knew all the midwives now and they greeted me cheerily, and I greeted them cheerily back because what else can you do? 'Hello again! Yes, bleeding again haha – what am I like?' I didn't want to be there, God I didn't, but as I was there, I was very glad to be cared for by people I already knew.

It didn't seem to be low-lying placenta. My placenta wasn't low now. The bleeding was worrying. They didn't know what was happening. I saw a different doctor every day and was told alternately that either it might be okay – they'd seen mothers bleed this much and still go on to have healthy babies – or, plainly, *this is very worrying; you are likely to lose your baby*. The certainty of either outcome changed constantly over the next week. On and off – hope and despair, hope and despair. Crying and sleeping and *not* moving – not an inch, moving might hurt the baby, just stay still – eating some Vimto jelly or sponge cake after every meal, taking iron supplements, laxatives, painkillers, not moving, going for twice-daily health checks with hours of emptiness in between, daily scans, infrequent toilet trips, changing pads, not moving, bad news, good news, well-meaning cleaning ladies telling me everything would be okay, that they were praying for the baby so everything would be okay, and hope, and despair, and hope and despair.

It was August 2020: visitors were strictly not allowed in hospital, due to Covid, so that week was spent alone in the hospital bed, oscillating between helpless crying, mindless boredom, hours of TV, and to be honest, plenty of laughing. It's hard to remain resolutely sad every second of the day and even though the situation was so very awful, it was a relief to laugh at times, and I am friends with some very very funny people. The support of my friends was amazing, providing sympathy and distraction and hilarity when each different thing was needed. And endlessly FaceTiming my husband, who was with me, in every way he was allowed to be, every step, heartbroken to be kept away, both from me, and the baby, and what was going on.

I had started to feel carefully optimistic, having been in a week; the baby's heartbeat remained strong, my waters hadn't broken and it seemed possible that with bedrest for a couple of months, it might just be alright. I was now 21 weeks. But that night, when the midwives came to do what was now routine monitoring of the baby, they couldn't find the heartbeat. Even then, I assumed it was just hard to find – it had been hard to find the day before but they had found it eventually. I reassured the midwife looking for the heartbeat. This happened yesterday, I said, but they found it eventually – the baby's just hiding. They smiled and kept looking but then they left to fetch a doctor. I'd never met this doctor before, and she came in and said, 'I'm very sorry to meet you in such sad circumstances.'

'I'm very sorry to meet you in such sad circumstances.'

It took me a few seconds to take that in. I mean, these are sad circumstances – everything's very up in the air; we're all very scared. Would she say that if things were as they had been all week – would you say 'sad circumstances'? No, you'd say 'worrying' or 'anxious', wouldn't you? Now, she's said 'sad'. No doctor has said that to me yet. 'Sad circumstances.' And that's when I realised what was happening. And everything changed.

She explained that my waters had broken, not suddenly at any given point, but gradually over the last few days, they now knew, from the scan. She explained that I would therefore go into labour and would give birth to our baby. She explained that the baby couldn't survive.

I was told the baby would probably come in the next couple of days. I would be put in a special delivery room for exactly these circumstances. But I couldn't go into it yet, there was another couple in there. Until I was in there, they said Marcus wasn't allowed to come and be with me – I was supposed to spend the next night and day alone, with the news the baby inside me was dying. Covid had made this whole process so much harder for everyone already but this felt a step too far. Both me and my husband were in bits, in shock and so far apart. In tears and shaking, I asked the midwife if they would make an exception – I couldn't get through the night on the ward alone. Thankfully they agreed, and Marcus came that night and we cried and we talked a little and we were quiet and we held hands and we were all together.

The next two days were . . . surreal, hard, powerful, painful, awful, intense, sad, loving. Once you become a patient going through this, you quite suddenly become cocooned in this web of people whose job it is to be kind and extraordinary. Midwives, bereavement specialists, consultants, nurses quietly descend on you to explain, to comfort, to help you.

At such a busy time, the people who looked after us never once made it seem like they were in a hurry, though they must have been. A consultant carefully explained exactly what would happen physically and tried to explain the biology of it, answering all of my many questions. Our midwife explained some of the difficult decisions we would have to make, saying we could change our minds at any point and quietly noting down the decisions we talked about. I was offered options for induction, options for pain relief. At a point where Marcus was going to go for a breath of fresh air outside, a specialist midwife literally ran after him to stop him so she could show him an alternative route downstairs, so that he wouldn't have to walk through the maternity ward and hear the cries of healthy babies.

There was a lot to do and so much to think about, but we felt so looked after during those days and in the months that have followed. We were given counselling and have been regularly in touch with our specialist midwife who was so kind and caring and has been a rock to us, even now. We are in touch with a specialist consultant who will help us through any future pregnancies, now we are high risk. It is hard to believe that this is these people's everyday jobs – to deal with the grief and sadness and various sensitivities around a baby dying, and that they treat you as if you are the only people on the ward. I have always felt grateful to the NHS but never more so than now. It has become an easy criticism of the NHS to moan about the layers of admin draining its budget. In a poll of a few years ago, Lord Ashcroft found that the public see 'too much being spent on management and bureaucracy' as the single biggest problem facing the NHS, and that they wanted to cut down on 'non-clinical staff'.[13] But it is this bureaucracy that arranges for grieving couples to access six sessions of counselling. It is this bureaucracy that liaises with baby loss charities who supply a memory box for every couple who have lost a baby, to take home with them. These non-clinical staff include cleaners, porters, canteen workers and bereavement counsellors. Those 'managers' are not stealthy besuited men in dark corners but, more often than not, doctors, nurses and consultants who have had to take on a managerial role alongside active shifts on the ward.[14] They are not 'taking money away from the front line'; they *are* the front line. The NHS provides a service that needs all those layers to help it function as well as it did for us, and we'll never forget what they did.

The day of labour I was full of oxytocin which, amongst more drastic effects, makes you feel happy, and it was sort of working. I felt more powerful than sad, and, after all, I had a job to focus on – a really clear and very difficult goal. Marcus and I distracted ourselves on and off listening to songs by Flight of the Conchords and watching Fry and Laurie sketches between contractions. At the moment the baby came, we held hands and stared into each other's eyes and cried.

The midwife, who had been with us all day and who delivered the baby, leant over and cried with us.

A little later, we saw and held our baby and said goodbye.

And the next morning, the real horror kicked in for me. Trying to find the word for it – the pain, sadness, trauma. Horror is probably closest to what I felt that day. The day after. For Marcus, he'd been painfully aware and alert all the day before but I'd basically been high as a kite and too exhausted and in too much pain to really take it all in. Waking up, with the drugs and hormones out of my system and nothing in my belly, I felt completely empty. My body felt pointless. I had nothing to show and nothing to hold.

When you lose a baby that you never got to know, you can't look at a photo of them, or treasure a memory or even, in most cases, talk to people about them. In the months leading up to this, mentally and physically, you've started to become a mother. You've put yourself in the category of 'parent'. But, after you've given birth, if the baby doesn't live, no-one knows that change happened – that you started being a mother. People look at you as if you are the same person as you were before. But you're not. You are a parent. You are a mother. But no-one knows.

Within a couple of months of our loss, two high-profile people talked of their own experience of miscarriage. I watched as Chrissy Teigen experienced something very similar to us – reaching the four month point where you feel confident in the pregnancy only to start bleeding, the hospitalisation, the oscillating between hope and reality and then facing the loss. She apparently had similar placenta problems to me and I found it all so sad to see it play out the same way. She posted stark, moving, tragic photos of her in the hospital when they found out what would happen. Meghan Markle also shared her miscarriage story in the *New York Times*. This was less specific – not saying at what stage or any details beyond holding her husband's hand and the cold white walls of the hospital – she said 'I knew, as I clutched my firstborn child, that I was losing my second'.[15]

These were well-known people who shared their stories, but thanks to the NHS, several baby loss charities and friends, I was also made aware of many more stories from women who had been through something similar to myself. And it really helps. It isn't just good for women going through it; it's good for everyone – to understand better, to be aware, to be better friends, colleagues, employers, family.

Both Chrissy Teigen and Meghan Markle were trolled on social media and shamed in the press for sharing their tragedies. Teigan was subject to thousands of monstrous tweets that veered between accusing her of narcissism, to saying it was fake. 'This has to be staged,' said one Twitter user, while another said, 'The hospital photo after losing your baby is about as narcissistic [sic] as you can get.' Another: 'She's just a cold ass bitch who is seeking attention.' Meghan Markle's revelation inspired Brendan O'Neil to write an article about how he doesn't think we should hear about other people's experience of personal tragedy.[16] Unaware of how much he sounds like a repressed Victorian husband, he ends the article by saying, 'Markle says that she and others have "opened the door", knowing that "when one person speaks truth, it gives license for all of us to do the same". No, thanks. We choose to close that door . . . leave us alone.'

So while it might seem like we live in a society where it is easy to talk about miscarriage, there are still many people out there who think we shouldn't or who want to police the way in which we do. We can tell our story but only in this one way that is deemed acceptable. There is still a risk for mothers – and fathers – in telling their stories; the risk of backlash, of being accused of showing off somehow, or wanting attention. In fact, there is value in sharing your story, if you want to. Whether those hearing it find solace in it because they have gone through it themselves, or they find knowledge and understanding of a topic they didn't know much about, there is value in sharing, for some. It can be healing to tell it and healing to hear it.

But also, the truth is, you do want attention.

I wanted attention for my baby. When you give birth to a healthy baby, they are showered with attention from family and friends. It is an event, a moment for everyone to share and it marks a big change in your life, and in theirs too. Unto us a child is born! It is a universally joyful and acknowledged thing. Something monumental has happened and it is talked about and remembered. When you lose a baby,* people feel very sorry for you, but you go back straight away

---

* I've chosen to say 'lose the baby' mostly when talking about what happened to ours. As things stand, the current terminology for losing a baby between 12 and 24 weeks is 'late miscarriage'. But many of us who have experienced it, and also many who work in that area of care, feel that the word doesn't really fit. For those of us who have gone through labour and given birth to a baby, who we've seen and held, it feels closer to stillbirth than miscarriage. Before 24 weeks, there is no birth certificate or death certificate, but there is a funeral and a name and a face. So we find ways to communicate our experience more clearly, in the hope that medical terminology might catch up.

to being just 'you', and no-one talks about the baby that you had, because it's too sad. And you want to talk about the baby. You grew it for five months and it came into the world and it left and what makes it worse is having no way to mark that happening. There's no grave or photos or memories. So yes, you want to mark it in some way, publicly. That's how I felt. After some time, I talked publicly about it, not in some selfless act of compassion, but for me, and for my baby. Look everyone – I had a baby. The impulse is still there, like any mother wanting to show off their baby. You have nothing to show people. No baby photos to post. You only have your story. So let us tell it.

As I write this, it's two months after the birth. We know more now about what happened and what the risks are for the future. We don't know if we'll be able to have a baby. Whether my body can carry one. Whether I'll be able to become the parent I feel I already am. It is a black cloud always there at the back of my mind. My feelings veer between acceptance of what happened and optimism for a future pregnancy. They veer between deep deep fear that I won't ever have a child and longing for the one I couldn't keep. They encompass hot, ugly jealousy of anyone I know who has children or is expecting a baby or has just had one, and then guilt for feeling that. Hope and despair, hope and despair.

The advice given on that card is familiar to me. 'What's for you won't pass you' is an old Irish saying. It's a nice thing to hear in certain circumstances. It seems hopeful on the surface of it – that something ineffable and all-powerful has an eye on everything and that when something passes you, it was never meant to be yours anyway. It works well as a reassurance for life as you forge ahead, and as a balm for afterwards, for missing out – it wasn't worth having in the first place, don't worry: something else, or someone else, will come along. It's both a consolation message and a well-wishing. But it works less well after an event like this, and yet, people say things like this to people who miscarry: 'it wasn't meant to be', 'it wasn't the right time', 'what's for you won't pass you'.

But it's not true. Sometimes what's for you, passes you. That's true for me, for anyone who's lost someone too soon, for anyone who wants children and can't have them, for anyone who doesn't have something that they know, for certain, should be a part of their life. Assigning a rhyme and reason to these things isn't helpful. There is none. Some things are simply shit. Unequivocally shit, and there's no silver lining. That's not to say that what you end up with, what you do have, isn't good and special and wanted. But sometimes things that were for you, pass you.

Whatever you do, do not sleep with ~~him~~ either of them

Most people have regrets about sex, don't they? Whether that is having had sex with someone who turned out to be awful or had sex that wasn't fun or had fun with someone who was awful or NOT had sex with someone who, while awful, would've probably been a lot of fun. Sex still feels important and therefore likely to inspire evaluation after the fact. Sure, it's become more casual for some people, but still more important than, say, having a sandwich or at least *some* sandwiches.*

Statistically, women are more likely to regret having sex and men are more likely to regret *not* having sex – having not made a move on someone and missed the opportunity.[17] Why do women regret sex more than men? I get why people in general might regret some of the sexual encounters they've had – if you can regret getting a blunt-cut fringe then why shouldn't you regret going down on David from accounts at Sarah's leaving party? But why do *women* regret the sex they've had more than men do?

I'm writing this chapter, which – ready the smelling salts – is going to be about sex, as a straight, cis woman who has only ever had sex with men, barring a brief encounter at an after-party for a production of *Grease* during which Sandy and Rizzo got on much better than they did in the musical. I've tried to be as inclusive as I can in what I'm writing, but a lot of it is rooted in my own limited experience. There's no doubt that outdated, restrictive attitudes towards sex affect every group and that a sex education that includes every

---

* There's an avocado wrap they make at Joe and The Juice that's so good it makes me cry. And, yes, yes, I am a millennial.

kind of sex and sexuality is beneficial to all. I'm not suggesting telling eight-year-olds about tentacle fetishes but that educating about sex, at any age – including adults – shouldn't dictate a 'right way' to have sex. As long as there is consent and an appropriate level of responsibility (in the words of Miranda from *SATC*, 'Wear a condom! S'all I'm sayin') then go for your life.

The Magic Number

I've had sex with quite a lot of people. I'm not being boastful *or* confessional in saying that; it's just true, and I don't regret much of it. A few perhaps – the half-remembered boy in Leith during my first Edinburgh Fringe in 2005, while sharing a three-bedroom apartment with 18 other performers, a tea-time shag for absolutely no reason and with absolutely no pleasure – I regret. The incredibly arrogant Italian doctor in Cap d'Antibes? No regrets. The sex was terrible to be honest but what a lovely view. But I've always been aware of my 'magic number' as the ladies' magazines used to call it. And phrases like that don't help – the idea that the number you've slept with is mystical and mysterious and holds any meaning; when what it is, mostly, is practical and largely irrelevant.

I think and hope that there's a younger generation now who are less aware and less judgemental of that number or at least judge men and women about it equally. But, for most people my age, there's still a back-of-your-mind voice-of-your-mother feeling that there is a limit to how many sexual encounters 'nice' girls should have, and it isn't applied to boys in the same way.

There may well be an emotional limit to how much casual sex anyone should have – it's higher than we used to think, less related to 'sin', but it probably still exists, because we're still human. By casual sex, we could be talking different partners or a fuck buddy arrangement (is that still the word?). The concept of

104

the 'fuck buddy' works well until you discover one of you cares more than the other does. I'm not saying that's inevitable but from my own experience, it is very possible. I had sex with someone casually for years, on and off, whenever we were both single, and for the first few years, I was denying that I really wanted more and it eventually made me sad, and then I think possibly the tables turned a bit and I ended up feeling like the bad guy for not wanting to commit. It's a difficult balance to keep without some emotional fallout and I think that's because sex still has an effect on you – whether it's a small effect or huge, and you can wear yourself out, mentally. And physically, I suppose, depending on how you're doing it. Spending 23 hours a day copulating is bound to be unhealthy – it doesn't leave you time to eat enough or clean the sheets. But also, there are purportedly more things to do in life, and it can mess up your head, and, like most things, it can turn into an addiction.

But I'm talking more about the societal limit on partners that is placed squarely on women. There is still, among many people, a deep-down, not-often-spoken idea that men are free to sow their wild oats (I still find this phrase disgusting, can't help but conjure up a man jizzing loose Quaker oats all over the floor of a mill) and that women should, firstly, protect their virginity and after that, keep a tight rein on how many people they have sex with. In spite of all the progress we've made in terms of women's rights and equality, there still exists, in some people's minds, the quietly held belief that men have more of a natural right to multiple partners than women.

In my twenties, I certainly felt worried as my 'number' got higher. If you're a young woman who isn't in a long-term relationship early on, who dates and who has short relationships of a few months and only the occasional fling or one night stand, it doesn't take long for that ridiculous, irrelevant number, to start stacking

105

up. And I can laugh now at what little difference that number makes. It hasn't made me feel 'slutty' or used or shameful for many years now but due to societal pressure, it did at one time, and I strongly suspect that doesn't happen for most men with the same amount of experience.

I am old-fashioned *and* I'm sex positive. I know I'm old-fashioned because I've reached an age where I don't always feel on the cutting edge of feminism. I think a woman can wear what, and as little, as she likes, and still isn't asking for it. But I haven't yet got on board with reclaiming the word 'slut'. I don't think I ever will. My goal is the same as those who would go on a slut-walk, but I think I'd prefer to just let those words – 'slag', 'slut', 'whore' – disappear; let them fade away into the history books and lose all meaning, rather than raking them up. But do I defend the right of any women to be as bare as a man without being deemed provocative? Yes, of course.

I still think sex matters, and I still think sex affects you. I've heard a phrase that goes 'every time you have sex with someone, you're giving part of yourself away' and that is ludicrous. How would that work anyway, after you've had sex a few times, what part are you giving them? A small toe? Half a spleen?

But I do think, to some degree, sex does affect you. The number doesn't matter. But each individual encounter does matter – it matters that you are safe; it matters that you meant to do it and that you enjoyed it.

Still to Come

I have very few regrets about the sex I've had but they mostly come back to the same regret: not figuring out orgasms earlier.

I started having sex at 18, and I didn't have an orgasm until I was 24 (as previously mentioned, I wasn't exactly on hiatus during those years). And to be clear, it wasn't the men's fault – they were doing a 'bang-up' job, some of them went above and beyond (and below and in front) in their quest to make me come, but it was impossible because I didn't know my body or how it worked at all. I mean, I knew how legs worked and where my elbows were – I suppose I should specify – I didn't know how my clitoris worked and had never really used it/practised on it/made full use of it. What a waste. Poor clitoris, sitting there watching sex happen and not getting involved. Like hiring Daft Punk for your birthday party and then getting them to play an acoustic set. Sex without the clitoris is a roast dinner without a Yorkshire pudding – it can be fine, but you'd complain to the pub if it was missing. I don't feel 100% comfortable comparing my clitoris to Sir Chris Whitty but, if sex *is* a government briefing, then, you just know it's going to go a lot better when Whitty is there and across everything. Next slide please.

I started being honest in relationships during these years and saying, 'Just so you know, I never have . . .' I thought this would take the pressure off but actually the opposite happened; when you tell some men you've never had an orgasm, they treat you like a wobbly shelf that needs fixing, and they're the hero to do it. I went from femme fatale to Unicef outreach mission in one easy step. I was to be rescued: I pictured them, down there, gearing up to save the day, adjusting the head-torch on their hard hat before delving in.

They were mostly good men, thoughtful and imaginative during sex and trying so hard but it was pointless until I'd found out for myself what made me tick. I'd find that every time I came to try, I was so in my head about it that nothing could break down that psychological barrier. As soon as I got close to the big moment, I panicked, and my body just waved a white flag and gave up.

After six years, I was resigned that it wouldn't happen for me – I was broken. This was just something I would never do, like knitting or the butterfly stroke.

107

So, here's the problem. No-one ever talked to me about female orgasm. We talked about male orgasm because that could get you pregnant. In sex education at school, we all had a big laugh about condoms and semen, but no-one ever talked about women coming. Not once. I went to a girls' school and was taught this stuff exclusively by women and no-one mentioned that the female orgasm was a) a thing or b) a thing that doesn't happen automatically. And it doesn't.

Things are better these days but not better enough. By the end of secondary school, the sex education curriculum teaches some important lessons that were missing in my day: consent, respect for your partner, that sex can have emotional repercussions as well as STDs and pregnancy (it was all STDs and pregnancy in my day), facts around miscarriage and the effects alcohol and drugs can have on your ability to make choices.

What is missing from that list, is teaching both boys and girls, that female orgasm is a crucial part of heterosexual sex,* and that it doesn't always happen easily and that sometimes you have to work for it. I mean, sure, some women DO come really quickly – a wink from a Timothée Chalamet, a Kate McKinnon or a 'The Rock' (depending on age/taste) and they're off. But for most girls, it's not something that happens immediately but something that you need to *practise* – like calligraphy or the Fosbury Flop.

I think it's worth telling young women of school age that they can start figuring that out for themselves on their own before having sex with a partner, while having sex with a partner or outside of having sex with a partner. It might seem obvious to some but it's not to everyone. It wasn't to me.

I want to mention the sex educators who ARE teaching these things. I opened up a conversation on Twitter about teaching

---

* It is, of course, a crucial part of lesbian sex, but in hetero sex, the male orgasm is often the overriding focus.

about the female orgasm and was inundated with replies, many from women who teach PSHE, studying doctorates in sex education or are professional sexperts, plus quite a few reply guys who waded in anyway. PSHE leaves room for interpretation by teachers so the wisest and most responsible are going far beyond the bare bones of the curriculum and finding imaginative, truthful and honest ways of explaining sex to students. Sadly, not many teachers are dressing up in giant inflatable vulva costumes with their head as the clit, as I had hoped, but many are being progressive and thorough in their teaching. One PSHE teacher talked to me about how even the definition of sex is geared towards male pleasure. Sex is often defined by the male orgasm, starting at male arousal and ending at male ejaculation and hopefully there'll be some other stuff in between, but that's extra. But as she said, that's why having LGBTQIA+ centred sex education is so important. If, from the start, you include same-sex sexual experiences, you see how ridiculous that definition is: the idea that you assign one person's orgasm as the defining one. It's important to teach sex as a process, not an act.

So, there I was at 24, having never done any of the practice or learning that I'm advocating above. I'd been having sex for six years and I knew perfectly well that I was missing out. And one day it seemed the right time to take action (I knew it was the right time because I had a solid three days off work and my flatmates were away – fate). I bought myself a vibrator from Ann Summers (many thanks, Ann), I stayed in bed for four hours, stopping and starting, trying to beat the panic and the fear, and just kept on keeping on, on and on, occasionally going numb, and then having to start from scratch, but persevering, on and on until – it happened. It. Was. Magnificent.

And once you've figured it out yourself and know your own body, it's much easier to introduce it into the bedroom with a partner. Not easy but easier. It's up to you how subtle to be – moans and groans and 'more' and 'less' do some work but aren't always as clear as you think. If you feel comfortable doing so, you can try things like moving their hand, showing them, pointing and, frankly, specifying clockwise or anti-clockwise.

The Question Of Virginity

I think a lot of sexual regret is still wrapped up, in a very old-fashioned crinoline bow, with the concept of virginity. And 'virginity', such as we think of it, doesn't really exist. It's a myth invented thousands of years ago and used in different cultures all over the world to shame women, to restrict women and to make ownership of women easier; it doesn't work anymore – it doesn't make any sense.

There's no doubt that high levels of respect towards virginity help to protect young women and girls in some cultures, but they shouldn't *have* to. Respect should be for the woman or girl – not for her sexual choices, or worse, a sexual history that has been forced upon her. We shouldn't need virginity as a safeguard.

There is no room in the concept of virginity for masturbation, queerness or female pleasure. The concept is flawed. The various meanings cancel each other out. It has traditionally, historically, meant the moment a woman's hymen is broken. This can happen riding a horse or using a tampon or just from a big shove. Can a girl become a 'fallen woman' by putting Dobbin into a gallop? Will she always remember her 'first time' with a Tampax mini? Ridiculous. Just as you can't define sex by when a man's orgasm starts and ends, you can't define 'virginity' as before and after a penis has been in a woman.

I'm going to focus more here on female virginity because female virginity and male virginity have always been used in totally different ways. Virginity for a man has often been seen as something to lose as soon as possible, a burden to relieve themselves of. There are many problems here too of course – all wrapped up in toxic masculinity that is so bad for men as well as women. The idea that sex maketh the man, that a real man is always up for sex and should initiate it and that sex should have little emotional effect on him, is damaging to men.

But for women, virginity has been used as a weapon. It has been something precious and important, to protect and preserve. Virginity for women has been intrinsically linked to their goodness, their value. And value is the right word – a woman whose 'virginity' was 'intact' was, literally, worth more – financially and socially, as a potential wife, as a potential prize, as an object. Girls who had sex before marriage or who had been raped were worthless – often publicly shamed, even put to death. This still happens today.

Let's take a quick look back at the ways virginity has been talked of in history, in a section I'd like to call 'this shit ain't new'.

This Shit Ain't New

Let's start with Greek myths. The goddess Persephone is abducted, raped and then forced into marriage by Hades, God of the Underworld. This is condoned by her father Zeus, as she is deemed his property – her virginity is his to give away. See how women's virginity is an object for men, well, male Gods here, to pass around between them – a bargaining chip, a business transaction or a gift between friends? 'Happy Retirement', 'Des! Here's some new golf clubs and my daughter's virginity – enjoy!' Once she's had her virginity taken, Persephone becomes a darker figure in Greek mythology, doomed to spend half her time in the Underworld. Her name among the Greeks became one used in curses. So far, so dark.

In Hinduism, the God Vishnu is the preserver and protector of the universe. Sounds like a great guy but in his backstory, he forcibly took Vrinda's virginity to get revenge on her *husband*, and, distraught at this, she threw herself on a funeral pyre and was reincarnated as a plant. And not even a massive kickass vengeful plant, like Audrey II in *Little Shop of Horrors*, but as a type of basil. Her virginity was used as a bounty in a battle between two men and she got reincarnated as a herb.

OK, moving from religious stories into real history now: how about the Vestal Virgins? In ancient Rome, a small group of women took 30-year vows of chastity, never married or had sex, and as priestesses, were imbued with a lot of power and influence. So again, there's the link that virginal = pure = moral = trustworthy and sexually active = soiled = immoral = untrustworthy. Celibacy is a positive thing if it's an active choice. But it shouldn't be the reason you get respect, and it certainly shouldn't be a condition of employment.

One of the most popular subjects I remember from school was the Tudors. Loved it! We were taught about Henry VIII at primary school as a fun, lively topic! Like an eccentric, ginger Father Christmas!* Elizabeth I, who became known as the Virgin Queen, was, at the time, slandered all over Europe by her Catholic opponents, as a whore. As an unmarried woman – the two versions of her were simple – virgin queen or illegitimate harlot. Meanwhile her supporters maintained she was pure and honourable and chaste. That was the best defence – that she was a virgin. The truth of course is likely the unacknowledged middle ground – she wanted independence but had a sexual appetite, making

---

* Just to recap, Henry VIII was a horny, morally bankrupt man who invented an entire religion so he could ditch his wife and marry the woman he fancied, who he then got bored of and had her killed so he could marry the next. Then he did that again two wives after that and kept going until he exploded of gout. No wonder his daughter Elizabeth I didn't fancy marriage all that much.

her neither a whore nor a virgin but a normal woman, albeit with slightly startling face makeup.

The whore/virgin dichotomy isn't just problematic, it's nonsensical. A supposedly 'promiscuous' woman can have had sex with thousands of people and, yet never have experienced the sexual pleasure that a technical 'virgin' might enjoy across a few splendid nights in on her own with a bottle of Rioja and access to the entire first series of *Bridgerton* on Netflix. You can be getting up to highest level kink, while still being a virgin, and you can have never known sexual fulfilment after having had a lot of penetrative sex.

Perhaps the greatest influence over the fallacy of virginity is the figure of Mary in the Christian Church. Even giving birth to the actual son of God – in a frigging stable, in a strange town, having to deal with untimely visits from strange men in hats trying to offload embalming fluid as a gift – wasn't a pure enough act of goodness to guarantee Mary's reputation. No, she was written up as a virgin. Just to make sure. It was vital everyone knew: She. Is. Nice. And the only way of showing that is that she's a virgin. And this handily spreads a message to Christian women too: this is the ultimate goal for you, ladies. To somehow stay a virgin but also have kids. It's tricky, I know, but Mary managed it, so . . . Somehow combining the two figures of womanhood that men of the time revered – mother and virgin. It is absurd and wildly unhelpful.

So, how does all this fit into the modern world? How can we possibly correlate the concept of virginity with today's women?

Let's roleplay!
'Hello, I'm Sally. Am I a virgin?'
'Is your hymen intact?'
'No.'

'Then you're not a virgin.'

'But I broke my hymen riding a horse when I was 12.'

'Well, then you lost your virginity to a horse. You must feel very foolish.'

'Hello, I'm Sarah. Am I a virgin?'

'Did you have sex?'

'Yes! I love sex! I came three times last night! With three different men!'

'Then you're definitely not a virgin!'

'Oh . . . we just did oral though?'

'Like the Blessed Virgin herself. God thanks you for your chastity, purest virgin.'

'Thanks Reverend!'

'Hello, I'm Grace, and I'm married to Paula. We have a great sex life. Are we virgins?'

'Yes, you are virgins! I think so . . . I mean . . . do you have penetrative sex?'

'Yes, sometimes; we mix it up!'

'Then no, you're not virgins!'

'But it's a piece of silicone, not a penis, so does it count?'

'Good point, you *are* virgins.'

'But I wear it, like, where a penis would be?'

'Errrr, I, well, I need to check this in the small print.'

'Okay, we'll wait. This matters to us.'

'Really?'

'Nope. Bye.'

It's such a confusing idea, it just doesn't work. If virginity is centred around the breaking of the hymen, you can do that without sexual contact. If it's centred around having something up your foof, you can lose your virginity via your own hand. If it's having jizz in your vagina, then couples who have used condoms for years are in fact virgins. If losing your virginity is just the act of having an orgasm (and let's be honest it hasn't been used to mean this, until very recently) then I was a virgin until the age of 24, in spite of having shagged many men since the age of 18.* (I'm bringing shagged back, what do you think? Very 90s, I know.)

And let's be honest, we don't mean first orgasm because, for many women and nearly all (?) men, that will happen during a 'special time' on your own, with no partner. No-one's going round suggesting that when boys furiously masturbate for the first time, in their rooms, over a poster of a young Nell McAndrew (very 90s I know), then they've lost their virginity.

Is loss of virginity simply the first time you have sexual contact with a partner? If so, where is the line? Heavy petting, top half? Frotting with clothes on? General caressing but you're naked? Oral? A light fingering? (so 90s!) Penetrative sex with a condom? Penetrative sex without a condom? Penetrative sex with a strap on? Anal sex? In those cases, at what point are you or aren't you, a virgin?

We can ridicule the notion of it, but the reality has serious emotional implications. Where does the idea of virginity leave rape survivors who haven't had sex before? If we use the traditional definition of virginity the way we've used it for years, then we are telling those rape survivors they have 'lost their virginity' through the rape. THEY have 'lost' it. Semantically placing blame on the victim and giving their experience a spiritual sounding significance on an act of violence they had no choice over. Suggesting to them that not only did they endure this terrible assault but that they have lost something irretrievable through it. Sure,

---

* If we use both penetration and orgasm as defining virginity, I lost my virginity at 18 and then again at 24. As Lady Bracknell might say: 'To lose one's virginity once might be seen as a misfortune, but to lose it twice looks like carelessness.'

115

you can recover from this trauma, but you can never get your 'virginity' back. It makes me very angry. What terrible, terrible bullshit.

If we really want to use the term, and I'm not sure why we would, then the best we can do is assign it to an inner feeling, defined only by ourselves. For me, I wouldn't give any one moment the dubious honour of defining the moment I experienced 'sex'. I certainly wouldn't give it to the dark, drunken, semi-consensual encounter when I first had a penis inside me. There are many more significant encounters than that, before and after it. If I had a virginity to lose, I lost it across an accumulation of experiences that let me know what sex could be like. I didn't 'gain knowledge' from that one moment. There was no single apple or forbidden fruit. There has been a smorgasbord of mixed quality fruit, eaten over a while. For some people, all that might coincide – your first time might be your first orgasm and your first love and all those things – lovely. For some women, I know virginity still holds some meaning. I know you may find it important, but I hope it is important to *you*, not to others. I hope that, for those women who feel something about their 'virginity', they own it themselves, completely. But for many of us, there are important and interesting watershed moments in our sex lives and the first time a penis enters you is far from the top of the list and deserves no special identity-defining word.

So . . . sexual regret.

'Don't sleep with ~~him~~ *either of them*.'

I'll never know the exact context the writer had for this – was it a warning to the rest of us – after they had in fact slept with both of them and regretted it? Was it a mantra to themselves, to avoid doing this in the future despite feeling tempted? Was the aim to not sleep with two different people on two different occasions or to avoid an ambitious polyamorous hookup?

116

I'm not an expert on sex. Not yet anyway, I did well at the coursework but flunked the exams. But I think sex should be enjoyed, not endured, and definitely not judged. That's not to say sex isn't a big deal. It can be, and sometimes it should be. Making healthy decisions about sex helps us. If you're reminding yourself not to sleep with him *either of them*, that might be good advice. It might be from experience; it might be instinct – good self-preservation. But if it's someone else's judgmental voice in your head making you feel that way, then fuck 'em. In fact, fuck ~~them~~ *both of them*.

All you need to remember . . .
Phone, wallet, keys

lip balm
mask
tissues
phone charger
face powder
hand sanitiser
2 tampons
chewing gum
a cereal bar
headphones
hairbrush
plaster
laptop
laptop charger
usb
scented candle
wood glue
vitamin B capsules
a spool
3 set squares
a poncho
dice
Ratatouille on Blu-Ray
a souvenir from Weymouth
smoked paprika
magnesium ribbon

shortbread
a working printer
baubles
someone's awful cat
an electric blanket
five gold rings
a quid
good sportsmanship
Eat, Pray, Love
barley
zips
Rupert Grint
your finest jewels
a fake fur
a Chesterfield
and a pen

Don't worry about things you can't control

I've got a lot of apps for my brain. Apps to help keep you on the straight and narrow, mentally and not let you slide into Bonkers.* Apps that keep you sane enough not to download the next five apps that keep you sane. There are loads of them now, and I've collected them all over the last few years.

I've got Calm, I've got Headspace, I've got Breethe.

I've got Mood, I've got Cove, I've got Mindful.

I've got one that reminds you to stop for a few seconds and stretch, one that invites you to write down the things you are grateful for and one that offers up a daily mantra in a soothing font on a stunning panoramic background.

> *'I am enough'* (on an image of a very large, old sequoia tree in a rich green forest)
> *'This too shall pass'* (dark thunder clouds receding into bright sunshine)
> *'In every moment, peace is a choice'* (on an image of a very still lake)
> *'Don't worry about the things you can't control'* (aerial views of an epic mountain range)
> *'Let it go!'* (spiralling frozen fractals all around)

The titular advice of this chapter fits perfectly into one of those apps and in an ideal world, it is unequivocally great advice. But, for me, and for many, it is very very difficult.

---

* I'll be using irreverent language to talk about mental health in this chapter, which I hope won't offend as it is my own mental health I'm discussing, and I find it helpful to really own my own bonkers/batshit/cray-cray.

One of the side effects of social media – self-publishing our every opinion and hearing everyone else's and the increasing ways we can now keep in constant touch with friends, family and people we barely know – is that a lot more stuff *feels* within our control. It isn't. But it feels like it is.

There's a petition to reinstate the right of British artists to work without a visa in the EU – I can control the Brexit Withdrawal Agreement!

My cousin just wrote a status on Facebook in sympathy with the incel movement and comments are open! I have the power to curb my cousin's misogyny!

Someone has posted a video of a Black person getting beaten by the police and I've retweeted it. I can improve the institutional behaviour of the Met!

I'm having acute pains in my chest and Google is telling me it's either a heart attack or indigestion. I can diagnose my own cardiac arrest!

We can now influence *some* things ever so slightly, but we can't, by ourselves, twice daily, take on the responsibility for ridding the world of the far right or improving Julia Hartley Brewer.

Before the internet, our news came in a digestible morning chunk, consumed perhaps over breakfast or on the train, and then if you wanted, once at night. It was manageable, we could listen to it, have a little chat about it, followed by a short think. If you felt strongly about it you could write to your MP or Anne Robinson on Points Of View, or if you felt very strongly, go on a protest march or go outside and shout into your shed, and then make your way to work/bed. But now there is more news every second with every screen refresh, and it feels very close to us and very much in our hands, literally and figuratively.

Don't worry about things you can't control.

It's very difficult.

In January 2019, I had what I like to call 'a nervous breakdown'. It's an old-fashioned phrase that I grew up with, something your parents might say quietly about an old friend of your Dad's.

'Sue said Terry's had a nervous breakdown' in hushed tones.

'No! I saw him last month; he seemed fine . . .'

I never really understood what it meant, and it isn't something I was ever diagnosed with officially, but I do think it fits what happened.

The *conditions* I experienced were anxiety and depression but the event – it was a proper event, it merited bunting – was a breakdown. And it was due to my nervous system going kaput.

Before I tell you about my nervous breakdown, I'll tell you about the year leading up to it.

A year earlier, at the start of 2018, I was living in the small, rented flat I'd lived in for eight years, a two-bed in Stockwell that I shared with a friend. My career was mostly in live comedy performing. I played to small gigs and clubs, around the country but more in London. My act was a mixture of standup and musical comedy. I was doing *Austentatious*, my improv show, too, monthly in the West End. I was also working in a primary school, playing the piano for a children's choir and doing piano, clarinet and singing tuition on the side. I was earning about £20k a year. I wasn't much of a party animal; I worked hard, ate a lot of ready meals and I was pretty content.

A few months earlier, in 2017, I'd got a job on a new weekly topical comedy show on BBC Two called *The Mash Report*, which was hugely exciting. My role was initially small. I would present the 'Social Media Wall' in a short, light segment, featuring fictional tweets from awful audience members called things like '@UKIPTony69'. My segment went down very well and halfway through the first series, from January 2018 on, I started to do more focused topical pieces, a longer section, and that I was allowed to co-write them.

The first piece was about sexual harassment. It came a few months after #MeToo, and it really hit a nerve/struck a chord/put the cat amongst the pigeons. I remember the day it was released online – I was in the production offices and my phone started dinging with Twitter notifications.

Ding! You've been mentioned 20 times.

Ding! You have 35 new followers.

Ding! You've been retweeted 350 times.

Ding! You have 2000 new followers!

Ding! Eric Idle followed you!

Ding! Paul Feig followed you!

Ding! You've been retweeted 5000 times.

And so it went on, all day.

By the end of the next day that clip had had 11 million views. By the end of the week, it had become the BBC's most viewed online content ever. Combining all my pieces for *The Mash Report*, they've now had over 100 million views. Things started changing quickly.

In December 2017, I had 95 new followers on Twitter.

In February 2018, I had 40,000 new followers.

It's only Twitter but 'going viral' changed things in real life. I was suddenly offered jobs I'd wanted for years – *Mock the Week*, *Q.I.*, *Live at the Apollo*.

In 2017, I had booked my own tiny tour of the UK with my show 'Keynote' (the tour that inspired this book!) to small studio theatres around the country, playing to around 50 people per venue, dragging my little keyboard with me on various trains to independent theatres and making about £100 profit per gig. In 2018, entertainment company Live Nation took me on, booked me a big tour of big theatres around the country, and it sold out within days.

Everything changed.

It was amazing.

It was terrifying.

One of the most heated receptions I got was in response to the controversial Trump/Morgan Mash Report clip. This was a clip referring to the presenter Piers Morgan's recent interview with President Trump on British TV, in which we criticised him for being sycophantic. It featured a cartoon picture of Morgan with his head literally up the President's bottom.

When that clip was released online, I was in an evening rehearsal, underground where there was no internet reception, and it went viral while I was out of reception. When I got above ground hours later, I suddenly had messages from my colleagues, my mum and several friends. It had spread across the internet but had also been very controversial. The texts ranged from 'Wow! This is crazy!' to 'Rachel, call me immediately' to 'Are you okay?'

I had personal emails calling me a cunt, Facebook messages from Trump supporters saying they hoped I got breast cancer (yes, it was specific) and intense trolling from British and American accounts – whether in defence of Trump, in defence of Morgan or simply against the filth of the image. I got called homophobic on *Good Morning Britain*. My parents were embarrassed by it and scared for me. I was tearful and afraid for weeks.

Needless to say, millions of people loved it.

I actually found a text exchange from the week it was released with someone in the business. The texts just about encapsulate everything I felt about working on *Mash* at that time. They said, 'Isn't this exciting?' and I replied, 'Yeah . . . it's a mix. It's really exciting but also quite scary; my agent's got me to re-do and double secure all my email accounts in case Trump's people hack me . . . it's all over the news . . . it's weird something I just thought would air at 10pm is now all over the USA, and my parents basically agree with Piers Morgan so it's been a tearful row. I'm fine as long as this is the peak of it.' I was crying for help but everyone else was just super excited for me.

I loved performing the shows in front of a live audience but the writing process was complicated. There was a very niche but important problem in my role on the show: that I was taken on as an actress to perform a small role written for me, and not as a comedian who gets control over everything they say. My role was always somewhere between a character and myself, and that 'character' was called Rachel Parris, so even if I was playing a character, it would be real life me getting the flack for whatever I said, and who would be responsible for it, as it was online, for the rest of my life. I wanted the same freedom of authorship that some other comedians got and added to that, and in spite of appearances, I was scared shitless of public reaction, whether I was *too* controversial or whether I was 'losing my edge'. I started to feel highly anxious about the work, the process, and the reception it got.

All that period of press attention during that series of *The Mash Report* happened at exactly the same time I got together with my now husband. We fell in love very fast, it got serious very fast, I moved in very fast. Once you're in your 30s and 40s and you know something's a goer, there's no point dragging your heels, and I don't regret any of how we did it – if anything I'd have married him sooner. But with hindsight, I can absolutely see how it was, to put it mildly, a lot. In the same three months, as my career changed completely from being unknown to being very in demand, I also started a new relationship, moved into someone else's house and suddenly had two teenage step-kids. It was a lot.

There is much that's wonderful about being in a blended family – not least my step-kids who I love very much. It must have been a lot for them to deal with and I'll always be grateful to them for letting me be a part of their home and their lives. Being in a blended family is also a lot about relinquishing control, for them and for me. In those early months, I was quite suddenly living in a 'home' that I didn't own or rent, which wasn't familiar to me yet, adorned with photos of a family I wasn't yet part of and a history I didn't share. I was the newcomer, so I didn't feel I had any authority within it. I felt lost. 'Home' still felt like the flat I had just left, which I'd rented for years and decorated and made completely my own. On top of that, step-kids are, at the start, children living in your home, (which obviously was their home first!), who you're really just getting to know, and any parental instincts you do have, you're not permitted to use. You have no rights. This is a family dynamic that already exists that you're just stepping into.

I felt very powerless. And that's how I'd felt in my career that year too. I think that 2018, which was outwardly my most successful and life-changing year, professionally and romantically, was a year in which I felt I had absolutely no control over my life.

Christmas Day 2018 was the day we got engaged. The proposal was cosy and romantic at the same time – a genuine surprise, and it happened while we were still in our pyjamas. It was absolutely wonderful and also; another big step. This was the first Christmas I had ever spent away from Leicester and the house I grew up in. The days across New Years, we spent at my new in-laws with my husband's extended family and had more family to stay with us after that. I had sensed something was coming, mentally. I felt completely overwhelmed and had begged for some space for just the two of us; I wasn't really coping.

On 5th January, the day when everything had settled back down after Christmas, we were sitting in the living room. Marcus was asleep in his chair and I was watching television and I suddenly couldn't breathe. I not only couldn't breathe but everything felt like it was pressing me out of the world. Evidently, it's hard to describe the feeling. A feeling I had then, intensely, and which would return again repeatedly over the next few weeks and months and occasionally since then.

It is a feeling like the world is ending but in a very physically compelling way. A feeling like I couldn't be here. It wasn't suicidal exactly, but more I just couldn't be here in this world – that something huge and awful was all around me and there was danger. But not in a vague, long-term way – in an immediate way, as if that thought was coming up your gullet, fast. It was fast. Like someone putting a hood over your face and everything going dark.

In that first moment it happened, I stood up quickly and walked around the room trying to find somewhere it felt better. There was nowhere. I opened the front door and stepped outside to see if fresh air helped. It didn't. I woke up my husband saying something was very wrong. I tried to explain. I couldn't breathe, and I was so scared. I'd never had a panic attack before. I think, even allowing for that, this was a severe one.

Marcus said he'd got me and that everything would be okay. He stayed calm; he helped me to breathe normally again, after a while. I came back to myself after about half an hour. I thought it had passed. But it happened again, a couple of hours later. I went from groaning like an animal on all fours to scream-crying in the bed while struggling to breathe. It was terrifying.

It just felt like my brain had snapped. 'This is what it is to be mad,' I thought. Days went on and it continued. Not constant but triggered by the tiniest things. A word in a song, a thought, a cold draft. Food was a trigger – I felt constantly sick and the panic about being sick made me have panic attacks when presented with any meal, so I stopped eating. Which didn't help my brain.

It was tragic as these were the days shortly after our engagement. They should have been filled with excitement and celebration, but they were filled with fear and sadness. I felt guilty about what it must have been like for Marcus to be with someone in this state – at this point I really was like an animal, trembling with laboured breathing and either crying or completely blank. But at the same time, and this was scariest of all, I couldn't feel any emotion. I've read up on it now and I know what chemicals cause it and all that, but it's absolutely terrifying – I lost all my love. And so, I lost any source of comfort. When I thought about Marcus or my best friends or my mum or dad, I didn't get any emotion. They were just names. It's not real, or rather, it doesn't last. It's a temporary chemical imbalance, to do with your amygdala's response to anxiety and depression. But it feels real.

We went to the doctor and he gave me beta blockers to stop the panic attacks. They helped. It went on, in that intense way, for weeks. The beta blockers stopped my heart racing, but I was still waking up every day feeling like the world was ending and with no attachment to my home or the people around me. I still couldn't eat.

The main emotion I *could* feel was fear. And I knew exactly what I was afraid of. I was afraid that I was mad. I was afraid that this was my life now – that I would always feel this blank, lifeless and weak, and that this was what madness was. And madness was me.

I started up with a therapist. I came off the beta blockers. I started eating solid foods. I started leaving the house. Slowly, slowly, things improved.

I think it must have been absolutely terrifying for my husband. He saw the woman he loved just . . . break. Instantly. Literally, one minute I was fine (stressed but fine) sitting watching TV, the next I was a ghost of who I was. Like the Dementors had appeared and fed on me while he was having a five-minute nap.

I was in a very lucky position when this happened to me. I had a partner to support me and a safe home to live in. I was otherwise physically healthy, so I was able to get to a doctor or go out on walks. I had a close network of friends who understood about mental health and were able to be a huge help. I had apps, beta blockers, talk therapy and endless online resources to explain and connect me with others. I can't imagine experiencing what I did, without a partner, a home, good friends, a safety net. And I feel lucky that it happened *now*, with our current understanding of mental health, rather than decades ago, when my behaviour would have almost certainly landed me in an asylum and provoked headlines like 'Hysterical Women's Libber Locked up in Loony Bin'.

Attitudes towards mental health are changing. Up until the 1960s and 70s, huge swathes of mentally ill people (suffering from a range of illnesses from schizophrenia to what we'd now call post-natal depression) were put into huge isolated Victorian institutions – hidden away from society and, therefore, easy to slip from the mind. The thought behind these institutions wasn't all bad. This was state-arranged care for the mentally ill that was organised long before the country had state-arranged care for the physically ill and when these patients were deinstitutionalized, the government essentially dropped the responsibility solely back on their families and away from professionals, which came with its own problems. If you're thinking 'quite right they dropped the responsibility back with their families' then consider whether you think that there ought to be provision for mental health, the way there is provision for physical health. If you do, then care is shared between family and professionals. You wouldn't expect such behaviour from an NHS hospital – suddenly saying this Intensive

Care patient is now your responsibility, bye. But on the other hand, putting a woman with post-natal depression in an isolated institution away from her family seems barbaric and is usually going to make everything worse. Whether you're talking about a passing bout of depression or lifetime of psychopathy – the treatment is different but the principle is the same. I think we are all working towards a balance between treating mental health in a professional way, but also with humanity. And acknowledging it exists, not hiding it away or running from it.

Don't worry about the things you can't control . . .

The thing I was worried about, in that dark time, was that I couldn't stop worrying. If you get anxious, you start catastrophising. Worries spiral until every small concern ends with the end of the world.

I feel sick . . . I can't eat . . . I'll never eat again . . . I'll starve to death.

The kids seem quiet . . . the kids are scared of me . . . the kids will hate me forever.

Marcus looks worried . . . Marcus is questioning our relationship . . . Marcus will leave me . . .

There's a hole in my sock . . . my foot will get cold . . . my leg will fall off . . .

It's very difficult when everyone is telling you to stop worrying about things that are out of your control, and you can't stop worrying. And so, you worry about the worrying. You worry that you can't stop worrying.

If you're in pain, particularly with heightened anxiety, your loved ones want you to stop worrying. It feels like the apps want you to stop worrying. Your therapist is asking what you're worried about.

What I started to feel was that if I continue to feel worried, I continued to be insane. Worrying = madness. And my greatest fear of all of this was being 'mad', *out of control*, batshit crazy. I felt batshit crazy and all I wanted, above all things, was to stop feeling batshit crazy. But I was still worried, so how could I recover?

In a way, what helped me on the road to recovery (and I did recover and I keep on recovering) was not so much the mantra:

Don't worry about the things you can't control.

But more:

Don't worry about feeling worried.

Sometimes feeling worried, even about things you can't control, is a perfectly reasonable, human response, and it doesn't mean you're crazy.

Do we worry about children, maybe your own children, no longer having access to free school meals? Of course.

Do we worry about the lives of people living abroad under dangerous regimes? Of course.

When a friend is making their way home at night, do we worry for their safety, even though it is out of our control? Of course.

Do we worry about hair loss, big tech, oncoming storms, and the mental health of the people on Love Island? I know I do.

And when you become part of a new family, are you worried that you won't fit in? That even if you're on your best behaviour, you'll never really feel part of it and you'll never be loved as an equal member in it? Can you control that? Not really. Do you worry about it? Of course you do.

But it's okay.

Don't worry about feeling worried.

One of the most important things that the apps told me was 'Check in with yourself. What are you feeling? Note what you're feeling. Don't judge it. Just be aware of it and gently move on,' all spoken in a warm American voice with a gently sibilant s.

So that's what I do now. I try to note my feelings without panicking about them. Even if that feeling is worry. There have been plenty of reasons to worry, for me, for all of us, in the last few years, so worrying isn't an irrational or paranoid response. But try not to be consumed by it; do everything you can to help yourself, and if you feel yourself panicking, start taking big   slow   breaths and believe that it will pass. All of this will pass.

You can never have enough tampons – stuff them everywhere!

I shall assume by 'everywhere' the writer means in your pocket, in your bag, in your office drawer, or tucked into a sock or a bra, rather than, as might be implied, in your ear, in your nostril, in your bum, one under each boob or a few taped into the armpits. Lord knows they are absorbent little guys and there might be some advantage to the latter in lieu of a good deodorant, but let's assume we are discussing easy access to tampons for period purposes.

Now, it's very possible, even in your mid to late thirties, to be caught out by an unexpected period. I know it seems like you should have it figured out by now but in truth, it can be unpredictable, and accidents still occasionally happen. Cycles can be irregular, sometimes very irregular, and periods usually give you a small lead-in before they get full-on – some spotting or smears so you can prepare yourself, but then, they don't *always* do this.

Periods sometimes take a short break mid-period, a day off for you with little or no bleeding (perhaps this is the day when we all go roller-skating like in the adverts) but again, you don't know how long that break may be or if that break is in fact the end of your period or if there's more to come – and that break may not happen at all – for many of us they're not always exactly the same because periods are sneaky and fundamentally Chaotic Evil.

And you can't just wear a tampon 'on spec', for just-in-case your period comes on a given day, because tampons are horrible to have in your foof* and painful to remove if you don't bleed into them. I'm afraid in spite of their long-term, and only recently declassified status as 'luxury goods', period products haven't yet reached a point where it's pleasant to wear them, especially when you're not bleeding. Tampons dry up your vagina and wearing pads for days can give you thrush. Mooncups don't dry you out as much, but even when you ARE bleeding, it doesn't feel hugely luxurious – you don't feel exactly like Zsa Zsa Gabor when you're doubled in half peering up your hole trying to insert a squishy goblet up there or mincing round the bathroom with a damp string dangling between your legs. I wish they *were* luxurious; I'm all for that. Tampons with a delicate Tiffany silver chain instead of string, panty liners lined with real silk, menstrual cups that double as a miniature champagne flute.

Speaking of luxury, period-pants that magically hold all your blood are an absolute miracle and even look nice – Always meets La Perla. They're an especially good solution for those days when your period may or may not come or is tapering out. But they're expensive, and you have to be able to put them in the wash within a day; you don't want them hanging around in your laundry basket.

So, the point is, periods can be surprisingly unpredictable, which leads me to the Udderbelly Stage of the Edinburgh Fringe 2016. I'm performing *Austentatious*, my improvised comedy show, in front of 400 people and wearing a light pink empire line dress. Mid-scene, sitting on a light pink upholstered chair (there were a lot of pastels in Regency times) I suddenly get that feeling: whoosh, my period comes. No subtle warning bleed – this has gone from zero to 60 and the 60 has gone straight into my unprotected pants.

---

* I am using the word 'foof' for vagina partly in homage to Caitlin Moran, and also because I find it funnier, more light-hearted than *vagina*, which sounds very serious. But really why is that? Why are we comfortable enough with penises that we find them easy to joke about but vaginas, vulvas, given their proper terms, sound oh-so-important and sombre? Why don't I find the word *vagina* fun? It's ironic, really, as mine really *is*.

At this point let me pause the action and lead you on a short journey back through the annals of time. 'Magical!' you're thinking. Yes, magical and also quite messy. If I had been living in the Regency era, as opposed to acting it out on stage, this would have been a very different experience. I mean, I suppose I still would have been unprepared for getting my period – menstrual irregularity transcends time and space – but even if I *had* had access to period products, those 'products' would have been a load of cotton rags suspended between my legs using a belt and girdle, and/or a few extra layers of petticoat.

Functionally designed 'sanitary' or 'feminine hygiene products' as they have come to be known, have been around for a surprisingly small amount of time, given that women have been bleeding for, well, somewhere between *Absolutely Ages* and 200,000 years. Period products only really got publicly acknowledged, designed and marketed in the 20th century, and there is still a long way to go before we nail the best practice for it.

Let's start with the language we've used to talk about periods. Back in the 1930s the terms 'sanitary napkins', 'sanitary protection' and 'personal hygiene' allowed ad men to market and advertise products without having to grapple with the uncomfortable realities of what these new products really did.

I wonder what alternatives were dreamt up in the boardrooms of advertising execs in those meetings:

'Clean-makers?'
'Softies?'
'Absorbos?'
'Too graphic Tom.'
'Fun-wads?'
'I like the "fun" angle, Tom, but I'm not sure wad sounds pleasant enough.'
'. . . cotton bullets?'

'Bullets are manly, Tom, use your head!'

'Lady-fillers?'

'That's a clever pun, but no.'

'Purity pillows?'

'I love that, Tom! Now we're getting somewhere!'

Ironically, in missing out on more descriptive language they vastly underplayed and under*sold* how life-changing these products could be for women. In the adverts for products like Tampax, Kotex and Pursettes in the 1930s to the 1950s, the words 'menstruation', 'period' or 'blood' are never mentioned. In fact, it wasn't until 1985 when the word 'period' was first used in a Tampax commercial, uttered by a young Courtney Cox, pre-*Friends* fame. Incidentally, 'I'll Be There For You' isn't a bad tagline for a tampon commercial.

Blue liquid in a clean glass jug was used for decades to show absorbency – it wasn't until 2017 that Bodyform (and in 2020, Kotex) used red liquid to demonstrate the absorbency of period pads. Even *the colour red* was too triggering for public consumption until a few years ago.

'Well, weren't they quaint and prudish back then?' I hear you cry. 'Haven't we moved forward! A toast to progress!' and we clink Mooncups.

Actually, the language around period products hasn't really changed, in a hundred years. The major manufacturers still call them 'sanitary towels'; the aisles of Boots still say 'feminine hygiene'. The term 'feminine hygiene' not only stigmatises women but excludes trans men who menstruate. These words might seem innocuous, but they're not because there is such a long history of periods being taboo and secret and shameful. This language isn't just vague and old-fashioned; it's riddled with unhelpful implications about menstruation, and it buys into well-trodden cultural tropes that say you are *un*clean, *un*hygienic, *un*sanitary when you are on your period. That has gone hand in hand with the idea that you should be excluded from normal activities until you've finished bleeding. This is still practised by some cultures around the world, for example the tradition of chhaupadi in Nepal where women are made to sit outside the village in unsanitised huts for the duration of their period. Such practices are backed up by all the major religious texts.* Meanwhile history books and art and literature have almost entirely ignored the existence of menstruation. It went – nothing, nothing, nothing, then *The English Patient* went WAY too far and ruined it for everyone.

It would be better if simpler, plainer language was used. 'Period products', 'menstrual products', 'pads' – these terms are clear, inclusive and don't make it sound as though anyone on their period is unclean and in need of 'refreshment'.

And while we're on the subject of language, I will continue to talk about periods on stage as a comedian because they can be important AND funny. That old stereotype about female comics endlessly talking about periods has never been true – I've never met a comedian who had more than a strong 20-minute set about periods – but if we menstruate, we will talk about it. Periods happen to many of us, often, and they can be funny or mundane, or difficult, and have complicated emotions attached and can have life-changing implications. Or, at the very least, can form the basis of many a good anecdote.

Which leads me back to the theatre, in front of 400 people in 2016, having just felt the blood drop. My obvious fear, as I sit there trying to stay in character and improvise a story throughout the scene, is that it will go through my pants, through my dress and onto

---

* I particularly like the bit in the Old Testament that suggests a woman should procure a couple of pigeons to say sorry for bleeding: 'But if she is cleansed of her discharge, she shall count for herself seven days, and after that she shall be clean. And on the eighth day she shall take two turtledoves or two pigeons and bring them to the priest, to the entrance of the tent of meeting. And the priest shall use one for a sin offering and the other for a burnt offering. And the priest shall make atonement for her before the Lord for her unclean discharge.' (Leviticus 15:28-30)

the chair, mid-show and that stain will be on the back of my pink dress and on the pink chair for the rest of the show; the cast will be disgusted, the audience will be horrified, many will try to leave, children will start to cry, a panic will ensue, the crying children will kick over a stage light that sets fire to our set, the theatre goes up in flames, and history will tell of the great tragedy of the Fringe all caused by one woman's failure to adequately predict her period.

That seemed the most obvious scenario, but it didn't actually end up happening. When it came to the end of the scene, I clenched hard, picked my dress up in a way that disguised what might be at the back of it, and looked back, checking the chair. Chair was clear, phew. I checked my dress in the wings, dress was clear, phew. I quickly rushed backstage and found our lovely assistant there who asked if I was okay and I said, 'I'm bleeding. Do you have a tampon?'

She did! She gave it to me, I did a classic emergency insertion, and I was good to go, but as I started towards the stage, one of our cast, Joe, poked his head round the door and said in an exaggerated whisper/mime 'RACH YOUR MIC IS STILL ON' . . .

So, apologies to anyone who was there that day and heard a dis-embodied voice utter 'I'm bleeding, have you got a tamp—' at which point they turned my mic off. It must have been a very surprising addition to the Jane Austen story you were watching but also a useful and very public reminder that indeed, you can never have enough tampons – stuff them everywhere, if not for yourself then for the sake of the next flustered, bleeding person who rushes into the room asking for one in a period emergency. You might really help them out. And, if you are ever the good Samaritan in this situation, go the extra mile and check if their mic is on.

Don't feed the trolls

This chapter delves into abuse on the internet: some of it pretty vicious and targeted, so if you think you'd not like to read about that, a) I don't blame you and b) skip this chapter. That said, if you are just completely unaware that ongoing online abuse exists in extremely violent terms towards particular groups, then, do find a way to educate yourself. It is useful to be aware that it happens, so that victims are believed.

'Don't feed the trolls' has been the go-to bit of advice for internet users for a decade now. The 'trolls' in question refer to the malicious and often anonymous voices on social media who churn out abuse to strangers. And to 'feed' one means to draw attention to, or respond to, these little pockets of verbal toxic waste.

Anyone who comes in for regular abuse online will have had 'don't feed the trolls' said to them often. But while it is well-meaning and has some truth to it, I no longer agree with it completely. For one thing, I think this advice suggests that if you don't respond the trolling will end – this is not always true. On top of this, I've seen victims of trolling blamed for responding to trolls, for somehow making things worse, when in fact I defend the right of anyone to respond to an aggressor if they choose to. It can be cathartic, or it can feel powerful to do so, even if it doesn't have the effect you want. It should be up to you how you deal with online abuse; you're not morally obliged to sit back quietly and take it. And finally, I know from experience that someone who seems like a troll can ultimately back down in the wake of being 'fed'. I have received some astonished and astonishing replies when I have responded to them, ranging from surprise that I ever read it, to surprise that I am a human with feelings, to, in fact, several heartfelt apologies.

This is by no means the norm, but I do think the internet is more complicated than it used to be, and a one-size fits all way of coping with online toxicity doesn't work anymore.

I'm even a bit sceptical about the word 'troll' because I think its meaning has changed too much to be useful. 'Trolls' used to occupy a small and specific area of online discourse. It was offensive tweets, vicious but rare, and people understood trolls to be a few people, mostly men, of a particular type, nerds perhaps, with no social life. And of very little agency. Just ignore them, people said, and still say, as if a troll were a fly that is somewhere in your house that you see occasionally, and you just don't want in your face. But, these days, with 192 million people on Twitter* and a billion on Instagram, trolling isn't a matter of one or two flies in your house but a swarm, ever-present, flying around your face trying to land and your nose is covered in jam. The idea of what a troll is has changed. It's not the anti-social boy in his parents' house; it's anyone. You can get vicious messages, tweets or comments from parents, from religious leaders, from professional journalists, from politicians, from teenagers or war veterans, from the left and the right. Sharp, furious, personal rhetoric has become so normalised that the meaning of 'trolling' has largely disappeared: where do you draw the line between trolling and, what is now, a regular, angry tweet?

I first started getting trolled when I presented *Thronecast*, a *Game of Thrones* fan show on Sky Atlantic. You might judgmentally imagine that the people likely to regularly watch and comment on a *Game of Thrones* weekly fan show, might overlap with the kinds of people to be online trolls, but that would be adhering to very limited stereotypes . . . and also prove to be largely true. #NotAllGOTFans. There was certainly a correlation between

---

* Interestingly, 66% of Twitter users are male. I wonder if the punchy, declamatory nature of Twitter attracts men more, or perhaps it is less attractive to women because of the regularity of online abuse.

the way viewers discussed the women on *Game of Thrones* with how they communicated with *me*. The sexualisation ranged from casual to shocking. To be clear, our fan show aired immediately after *Game of Thrones* itself aired each week, on the same channel. So, viewers and fans would tweet us – the fan show, and me and my co-presenter – their comments about the latest episode, as well as comments on us and the fan show. They'd tweet using the fan show's Twitter handle, our personal Twitter handles and/or all the official hashtags attached to the show itself. So basically, we saw it all in its grimy reality. Yes, *Game of Thrones* features sex a fair bit but the comments about the show wouldn't always be talking about the sexual scenes. Large numbers of men commented on the shape and colour of Cersei Lannister's pubic hair during her dramatic and emotional 'walk of shame'. There were many innuendos made about the women on the show receiving a 'Littlefinger', which is the name of one of the male characters, and one man, shockingly, saying that Caitlin Stark's slit throat, during the Red Wedding, looked like a vagina. Pretty harrowing.

The comments directed at me ranged from sexual to complimentary to aggressive and nearly always related to my appearance, ranging from being called 'a blonde cunt' for mispronouncing a name in High Valyrian, to one guy creepily enquiring about the 'nice bruising' on my leg and how I got it. I was known to many simply as 'the blonde', even to viewers who had tuned in every week and were tweeting that they missed me on the show. Here are some real-life examples:

'Thronecast can fuck off, blonde bitch doesn't know anything bye'
'@Jamie East – you and the blonde girl were great!'
'Thronecast is shit these days. Bring back the hot blonde and good tv'
'What happened to the blonde chick whose been replaced by Sue Perkins?'

'blonde girl on Thronecast is the most annoying person ever to appear on TV'

That really packs a punch. According to this tweet, that makes me more annoying than Louie Spence, Paris Hilton AND Mr Blobby. Mark me officially wounded.

Some did learn my name:

'#fuckoff Rachel Parris and go back to being Girl In Café and stop telling me what I've just seen'

Unfortunately, telling the audience what they've just seen in a post-show fan programme was *very* much my job, so I wasn't able to take his criticism constructively. For those wondering, 'Girl In Café' was the last sitcom role I had done, which makes me think this guy was so furious at me for telling him what he's just seen that he bothered to look up my IMDB profile just to inject some archival information into this tweet.

Some featured a huge tonal shift halfway through:

'I hope the bastard of Bolton pisses on your ankles Rachel Parris but that's a nice dress you're wearing tonight – [flowers emoji]'

Talk about mixed signals. But largely the tweets were casually objectifying. Not overly offensive, just a stream of comments on my appearance (the like of which my male co-host Jamie East, never received). There seemed a particular fascination with my legs, which I found odd as I have a totally unremarkable pair of legs.

'After watching Rachel Parris in Thronecast, I just have two words 'Those legs' wow'

'Just watched Thronecast and found myself hypnotised by Rachel Parris legs'

Disclaimer: my legs hold no coercive powers.

'Miss lovely legs'

'I swear those legs are getting longer'

Update: they weren't.

Even just friendly comments from genuine fans on the show would, as if it was a box to tick, always include a passing comment on how I looked, sandwiched into a comment on the plot.

'What an episode! Rachel Parris looking lovely, digging the curls. Shay shafting Tyrion – what a role reversal!'

It was a fascinating introduction into the world of being a woman on television, and I experienced it in a little-known show and as a white straight woman talking about a fantasy programme. Imagine the backlash if I wasn't white and young, and if I talked about politics and didn't have the ability to – what was it – hypnotise people with my legs? That's definitely going on the CV btw; I'm sure it's a transferable skill. These comments were pretty gross and made me feel uncomfortable but were minor compared to the horrendous abuse many women in the public arena face every day.

Labour MP Diane Abbott is the first Black woman to ever be admitted into British parliament, and the longest serving Black MP – serving Hackney since 1987. Throughout her career, she has been subject to sexist, racist and sizeist abuse. In the lead up to the 2017 election, Amnesty[18] found that she received almost *half* of all abusive tweets directed at female MPs.* The viciousness of the tweets towards her are breathtaking – and provoked simply by her existing as a Black woman in politics. Tweets included calling her 'fat', 'disgusting', a 'parasite alien', 'bitch' and using the n-word and the r-word.

Another Labour MP, Jess Philips, has been targeted by trolls calling her 'fat', 'ugly' and 'common', but her abuse became even worse when, in 2016, a UKIP candidate, Carl Benjamin, tweeted that he 'wouldn't even rape' her. When she complained about this, she started receiving hundreds of rape threats from men on Twitter – up

---

* The same study showed that Black and Asian female MPs received 35% more abusive tweets than white female MPs.

to 600 in a day[19] – and became a target for the 'You can't say anything anymore' brigade.

It is hard on those thousands of men who now feel less comfortable about publicly stating who they would and wouldn't rape. But one consolation for the 'You can't say anything anymore' crew is that you CAN say anything anymore and get away with it! Hurray! Freedom of speech is maintained! In evidence of this: when questioned about his tweet, Carl Benjamin just doubled down on it a month later saying 'There's been an awful lot of talk about whether I would or would not even rape Jess Phillips . . . I suppose with enough pressure I might cave, but let's be honest, nobody's got that much beer.' To be clear, there have been no legal repercussions for his repeated public discussion of whether he would or wouldn't rape Jess Philips – he's fine, lads! And cherry on the cake – misogyny still isn't legally classed as a hate crime.*

Benjamin and his defenders claimed that it was just a joke, and you can't legislate against jokes. I suspect he is exactly the kind of man who can only empathise with a cause if it directly affects him, so I wonder if he would consider it a joke if a grown man said he 'wouldn't even rape' Benjamin's daughter or his wife. I wonder if he would laugh, if he would add it to his list of 'extremely funny English jokes for traditional manly men to enjoy' that he pulls out in the pub to entertain his mates. We can't know, as he has certainly never delved that far into self-examination except perhaps to ask questions such as 'do I really like craft ale?' or 'am I gay if I fancy Nick Griffin?'

In the same controversial tweet, Benjamin also said 'Feminism is cancer'. Speaking of cancer, I received the following message in my Facebook inbox after I did a humorous piece on *The Mash Report* about Donald Trump:

---

* With much campaigning from women's groups, it got as close as it ever has in 2021 but, at time of writing, has not passed into law. Hardly surprising when people like, say, the Justice Secretary Dominic Raab, don't even know what misogyny is. He said 'misogyny is absolutely wrong, whether it's a man against a woman or a woman against a man'. Screams silently.

Lady you are a nasty, despicable pig and chances are that Karma makes you suffer dearly for your unfairness. Better get that mammogram early!

This is from an American account called John Smith whose profile picture is of a cuddly Elmo from Sesame Street. Aw! Hard to imagine a more targeted attack on a woman than wishing her breast cancer, but ultimately the joke's on him. Thanks to his health warning, I WILL get that mammogram early, and while I'm at it, an up-to-date smear test as well! Thanks, John!

Trolling is so *normal* now. You don't have to look far, it is everywhere and the reaction when people talk about it is often 'just ignore it' or 'well, you're the one choosing to be in the public eye'. This argument is perhaps the most absurd in modern discussion. When you order a beer at the bar and the barman pours it over your head, you don't think 'well I did ask for beer'. If a BMW suddenly mounts the kerb and runs you over while you're walking that's not okay because 'you know what, it was my choice to come outside today'. If you went to a P!nk concert and during one of her aerial stunts she suddenly unzipped from her harness while dangling directly above you and, with intent in her eye, dropped herself right onto your head, while singing 'Raise Your Glass', you wouldn't think 'you know what, I was asking for that when I bought the ticket'. Okay, enough examples but you get the point. Some people choose to be in the public eye, some people don't but are thrust into it anyway, and in either case they are not 'asking for it' when it comes to abuse. That's not part of the contract.

I did a report on incels for *The Mash Report* in 2018. The incel community is a large and growing set of online groups made up of disenfranchised and potentially dangerous men. They often attract rather lost, underconfident men looking for friendship or support and radicalise them. Incel is short for 'involuntarily celibate' – these men define themselves by their lack of sexual success with women, and blame all women for that, as well as some other, more sexually active, men. While often masquerading as male self-help communities, at their heart, they are virulently misogynistic. Beliefs that are perpetrated by many in these groups include that sex from women should be forcibly shared out among men so that no man has more than another, and no man goes without: to be clear, enforced large-scale rape. There is a language used by many of the communities such as 'femoids' or 'foids' for women – marking them as inhuman. Their hatred of women goes very often hand in hand with beliefs in white supremacy, racism, anti-Semitism. The incel community is responsible for inspiring the actions of young men such as Elliot Rodger who murdered six people in 2014; his planned target were sorority girls, part of the society that had 'denied' him sex and love.

I was keen to do a piece about this growing threat. I was happy with the actual video we made but I was nervous about it coming out online – I tried to be very careful and specific about how it was packaged for online release.

I didn't seek out reactions to the piece at the time beyond the ones I'd ordinarily see on Twitter and Facebook but it was two years later, after reading Laura Bates' extraordinary book *Men who Hate Women*, that I decided to have a look online to see whether there had ever been a reaction from actual incel websites to that piece I did. I simply googled Rachel Parris incel and the first accessible incel site I came to (most have security checks to get through) Incels.co, had the following about me from that piece in 2018:

Some of this uses very upsetting language – of violence, misogyny and anti-Semitism – so do skip a page if that might be triggering.

'Rachel Parris is her name, in case you're wondering.' (With a screen-grab of *The Mash Report* video.)
   'Cunt. Not one second.'

'I searched her name on youtube and the literal third video is men-struation-comedy. Whatever escapes her mouth could only be shit'

'fucking whore, I'm not gonna watch though'

'She's an ugly Jew who needs to be gassed. Enough said.'

'She knows how to suck her Jew master's cock; shiksa whore' (with a screenshot of a tweet I wrote about anti-semitism)

Two photos of me and my husband, taken from my Instagram, posted without comment.

'All foids need to be skinned alive'

'Someone should shoot her in the tits'

This was only the first incel site I found, the first easily accessible one, and I didn't keep looking. I felt a bit scared for the first time. The photos of my family, the incitement to look me up online, the gendered violence, of course, and not to mention the slightly unexpected anti-Semitism – useful to note you can be abused as a Jew even when you aren't one. Racism truly knows no bounds.

'Don't feed the trolls' doesn't work as a piece of advice because the truth of online abuse is simultaneously broader AND more niche than 'trolls'. Trolls aren't a tiny group of harmless lonely men in the basement. 'Trolls' now range from candidates for European Parliament, to ordinary people who are so passionate about politics that they veer into death threats, to underground groups of young men so brainwashed by misogyny that they have murdered large groups of women. Incel culture is very real and a growing threat to women. In everyday online discourse, violence has become normalised. Insults have become normalised, sexualisation has become normalised.

And there's such a wide variety – trolling, if we use that term, can happen to anyone, famous or non-famous, man, woman, non-binary, trans, Black, white, biracial, jewish, socialist, disabled, athlete, political, musical, talented, untalented, outspoken, academic, left-wing, right-wing, vegan, carnivore, YouTuber, florist, juggler, mother, child, train spotter or Rylan. Anyone is fair game. And what is shocking is that a lot of trolls really don't think of themselves as the villain. They think they are in the right, and they're fighting injustice or campaigning for common sense. They are angry and feel justified in what they say. That's what's scary. Most trolls now aren't random sociopaths. They're just people. And they're not hiding. They're in the open, by choice, because they think they're right.

So not feeding them isn't a solution. It might work for some, but it's not a cover-all for most online abuse. Just ask Jesy Nelson, Rachel Riley, Nish Kumar or Rosie Jones if the fat-shaming or anti-Semitic or racist or ableist abuse they get happens only when they respond to it. Clue: it doesn't. It happens anyway.

So, I'm not saying respond to all trolls. Sometimes the answer is to save yourself the angst, to step away and try to find some peace from it. And sometimes you want to fight back, to share, to shame, to howl at the moon, to give them a rhetorical slap, an online spanking or, my favourite, an eloquently worded reply that indicates that I'm not angry, just disappointed.

Read more, read endlessly, motherfucker

I would add to this: read books. [motherfucker].

It's easy to read: blogs, quotes, tweets, Facebook statuses, over-written billboards, film reviews, a worn-out Metro newspaper, the egregiously friendly customer service witticisms on the back of your smoothie bottle. It's so easy and it feels fast and busy and part of the everyday and keeps your mind whirring along with what's going on in the world and who's doing what and what you should be thinking about and who you should be in touch with and what to eat and how your child compares to theirs and what you need to order and where to go when and who why with who what are they thinking should I think that oh now I do or do I but there's something about reading an actual book that makes you slow down.

I think it's getting harder to commit to a book. Especially if you have a busy life, a stressful job or a family to look after, and now there are a million other things to look at instead, and after a long day who doesn't just want to stare at *Parks and Rec* repeats until you fall asleep or play Candy Crush for your entire commute until your hands cramp? Our brains are changing, our attention span is changing.

But reading at length is special and it really is good for you. Research has shown that reading books involves a complex network of circuits and signals in the brain. As your reading ability matures, those networks also get stronger and more sophisticated. The same study found that reading fiction increases your empathy; long-term fiction readers have a better ability to build, navigate and maintain social relationships. Reading books can make you a better partner, friend, parent.

But mainly, it's fun! It's so wonderful, to escape into another world for a while. To be in someone else's mind, a different type of society or a different time, a different job, to feel wrapped up in it, to follow a narrative, a feeling, a culture that is not your own, to invest in someone else's story. You learn so much from reading books but also, and more importantly, it is joyful.

Endlessly joyful. [motherfucker].

Follow your dreams

1. What are they?
2. Don't.
3. Stop it.

Now, I'm an optimist, a romantic and a dreamer. I love dreams. Not actual dreams – my actual dreams are very, very boring. Really, painfully dull. I often dream about trousers or groceries, going down some stairs or eating ready salted crisps, but goals, ambitions, huge madcap plans? I'm all for them. Reach for the stars, aim high, spread your wings, think big, boldly go where no man has gone before. I really agree with all that. But following your dreams is a bit different. Dreams are, by their very nature, a bit vague, out of reach, unrooted and blurry round the edges, much like my email inbox. Dreams need pinning down in order to follow them, and, at that point, they cease to be a dream and become a plan. And I believe you shouldn't follow a plan you decided on years ago at a younger age with less information than you now have – plans should change depending on what happens to you. And what if that thing you've 'dreamt of' isn't the right thing? What if it isn't as fun or as exciting as you thought, or you're not actually that good at it, or it doesn't end up bringing you as much joy as expected? When I was six, I wrote to one of those make-kids-dreams-come-true programmes asking them to show me how cheese is made.* That was my big childhood wish – to see up close the protracted process of separating curds and whey and the slow noble art of maturing cheddar. That's all I could dream

---

* Yes, yes, it was *Jim'll Fix It*, and even he thought my dream was too boring to feature on the show.

up at six – and nope, I wasn't even a cheese obsessive. I just *quite* liked it. What if the thing that you could potentially really love doing and being *isn't* your dream because you haven't thought about it enough yet, or don't yet know that you can do it, or it doesn't exist yet? You have to leave room for the possibility that The Dream you've held on to and nurtured and held in your heart for years might be . . . wrong.

The job I do now – which is a comedian, or 'so-called comedian' according to @britishbigballs69 on Twitter, has never been my dream. I never expected to be a comedian and no-one else would have expected me to be a comedian. Not. in. a. million. years. No-one thought I'd be one and lots of people wish I would stop. Not least my mum and Piers Morgan. And they've never even met. I suspect they'd get on.

I would never have thought of comedy as a 'dream' option. My dream was to be in musical theatre or in historical period dramas on TV. I knew about both of those things. I'd seen them. I'd been taken to see *Les Misérables* when I was about six, and I'd watched a lot of Catherine Cookson costume dramas on the telly growing up. I knew I liked performing, but my particular dreams were totally shaped by the types of entertainment I'd been exposed to by the age of 16 – influenced by the tastes of my parents and what was playing at the Leicester Haymarket in the mid-nineties. So that became my dream – to be in the chorus of a musical, or to play the rebellious daughter of a rough-talking steelworker in 1920s Middlesborough.*

But as I've got older, my dreams have kept changing. For one thing, TV stopped making Catherine Cookson adaptations, more's the pity. But also, I came to know myself better – what

---

* There's always one of those. I have all the Catherine Cookson adaptations on DVD if you'd like to borrow them; I think they're tremendous. *The Glass Virgin* was a particular highlight, starring Mr Higgins from Downton as a renegade Irish-Spanish horse trainer.

skills I have to offer, what I enjoy – and I also realised there were many more versions of being a performer than I'd ever known about: improviser, musical comedian, online satirist, sketch-writer, burlesque artist*. . . Now that there were more possibilities, I needed to re-evaluate my dreams. And I keep doing it. I now know I much prefer performing my own stuff, creating new things and the freedom of doing lots of different kinds of performing. A Jack-Of-All-Weird-Trades. Also, I can't learn dance moves for shit. And, instead of being in a period drama on TV, I started *Austentatious*, an improv troupe who dress up in Regency costume, get a made-up title from the audience and perform an improvised Jane Austen story on the spot.[†]

We've done this in the West End and all over the UK for 10 years. If I followed 'my dream', even in the best-case scenario, I'd have only got to play Lizzie Bennet once, probably in a low-budget ITV version with none of the class of the 1996 masterpiece. As it is, I play a version of her every week, surrounded by my best friends, and it's different every time, from my *Game of Scones* to my *Empire Line of Duty*.

My point is not to damp down your ambitions, but the opposite – don't tie yourself down to one idea when a whole load of even better, funner things, could come along, things you might not have thought of.

Take Zoella, she's a multi-millionaire YouTuber. She's great at it – a talented make-up artist and, for all the judgey uncles who used to scoff about YouTube as a profession – 'Absurd! Our niece wants to be an u-toob-ster? What on earth? Why can't she have

---

* I performed in a burlesque show at my first Edinburgh Fringe, receiving a one-star review that said: 'The only thing that can be relied upon in this painful hour is that not a single performer on stage has ever experienced orgasm.' Which was, at it happens, bang on the money. See chapter 'Don't Have Sex With Either Of Them'.

† Things like *Strictly Come Darcy*, *The Empire Line Strikes Back*, *Bennett Like Beckham* or *Dial Emma For Murder*.

a proper career like a baker or a miner or a carpenter? What's wrong with going down the pits, Maisie?' – well, scoff at this: Zoella has the fastest selling debut novel in the UK beating JK Rowling and E. L. 'Fifty Shades of Grey' James.[20] Now, I think she's probably living her dream life BUT this would never have been her 'dream' job, because this career didn't *exist* when she was a child. It wasn't a thing. She helped to invent the concept of a 'YouTuber'. So instead of following a dream, she conceived a whole new thing and excelled at it, and now, that is an ambition for lots of other children – kids aged 12 are now three times as likely to want to be a YouTuber than an astronaut. Judgey uncle wouldn't enjoy that statistic either. 'They'd rather be splattered all over the goggleboxes than go to the moon nowadays Jill! What's happened to our young? Why don't they want a sensible job like exploring the limits of our solar system? What's wrong with being a good old-fashioned astronaut, Maisie?!'

I joined an improv troupe when I was 22 and I learnt that improv is all about saying yes. To help prove my point, I didn't sign up to join this improv troupe myself, my friend signed me up secretly and took me to the audition and sprung it on me. I just said yes. I got in, and it changed my life. I'd never have thought of myself as a possible comedy performer until that happened and it happened because of an unplanned and unexpected offer.

In improv, you say 'yes, and'. Someone offers you an idea, a character, a scenario, you say 'yes', and then you take that and you build on it, and then they say 'yes' to what you've built, and you both just keep building and building until you've got the makings of something funny or interesting. 'Yes, and' is an ethos that is helpful for everyone in every walk of life,* whether it's in

---

* Check out Pippa Evans' brilliant book *Improv Your Life* for more on this.

corporate Zooms, PR brainstorm sessions, interviews, auditions, writing rooms or awkward PTA meetings. The key isn't just in the 'yes', but also the 'and'. It's about listening to what's on offer, being open and positive, and then creating your own thing from it. And I think you can find opportunities in the strangest places by saying 'yes, and' more.

Now, that's a tricky lesson, especially for women. As a feminist, I'm cautious in suggesting women should say 'yes' more – it's steeped in problems because we are asked to say 'yes' much more than men are. We are expected to acquiesce more often. We are asked to smile and to bring a positive, friendly vibe. That's not what I'm talking about here. I'm not advocating saying 'yes' to menial jobs that your male counterparts can't be arsed with or saying 'yes' to wages that are beneath you or saying 'yes' to behaviour that is unacceptable or saying 'yes' to every job you get asked to do, even if you don't want to do it and you get a smug high from over-working yourself, living with exhaustion that results in a catastrophic mental breakdown from burnout. Been there, done that, not recommending it. 'No' has its place; it's vital. But I believe that we gain a lot from sometimes saying yes to new experiences that you may not have dreamt up.

With a lot of this, I'm talking about work. Saying 'yes' to jobs that might not appear to be on the ladder to your 'dream'. They can't all be, but you have to work, you dreamy weirdo, so go and earn some money. And who knows, one of those jobs might actually turn out to be a great thing – you might end up wanting to do that instead. Or it'll just keep you afloat while you work on your other stuff. Either way, you have to get a job. One big one or lots of small ones. You have to pay the rent. Unless you're a Laurence Fox type with an apparently endless stream of money or influential contacts from your dynastical family, pursuing dreams is often a pretty low-income affair. Whether it's studying for a veterinary degree, saving up for your own salon, interning at a big magazine, auditioning for acting parts or trying to be a comedian, you'll need to pay your way as you go.

Finding out what your dream should be is a long game and you have to keep working while you do it. Between leaving university and going full time as a performer (which was a gap of 13 years), I had many different jobs – some part-time, some full-time, some over-lapping, some freelance – ranging from hotel lobby pianist to shop assistant and from cocktail waitress to financial administrator at the Royal Opera House. I had range. Full disclosure, within a month at the cocktail bar, I was demoted from making cocktails to serving 'mixers and bottles' as I was so bad at remembering what went into them. Nonetheless, I think you learn something from nearly every job you do, whether it's how to fill a spreadsheet to how to make a proper Old-Fashioned.* And I can honestly say I'd never have found out about all the things I love doing now, or known how to do them, without doing those jobs.

Going off the dreams path a little but here's a really boring but important bit of related advice: learn how to do admin. Whatever you do – pop star, accountant, painter, lawyer – you will need to be good at admin. Everyone has to be. The only point at which you don't have to be good at admin comes when you are so rich you are willing to cede complete control of your career over to other people and that's rarely wise and can result in a Britney Spears-type situation.

Here are some things I've done, as part of my job as a performer:

Constant stream of emails – seeking, accepting and confirming gigs
Keeping a tight diary

---

* Bourbon, brown sugar, cranberry, lemonade, vodka and Apple Sourz, if memory serves.

Negotiating fees

Writing, sending and chasing invoices

Filing invoices so I know when I have and haven't been paid

Keeping an expenses report

Filing tax returns

Hiring photographers and designers to create flyer and poster images

Sending those images to magazines, websites and promoters

Sending those images to printers

Receiving thousands of posters, separating them into appropriate numbers to match theatre capacity, rolling them up and posting them to various theatres round the country

Finding and contacting local websites and news sources and radio stations to ask if they'd help promote my show (they often will)

Building my website

Maintaining my website

Booking tour accommodation

Booking trains in advance so you don't pay more in train fare than you're getting for a gig

Doing unpaid podcasts, interviews and articles for various publications in the hope it might sell you an extra ticket

Filling in applications forms for festivals and competitions

So. Boring. But. Necessary.

There comes a point where some of those jobs can get handed to someone else to do, but that's a choice and it comes with its own admin. You're then employing one or a team of other people to work for you; you still have to give notes and approval on every artistic choice, reply to the same number of emails, you have to set up a payment system for them, negotiate what they're getting for doing that job – a fixed fee or a percentage and check if you're still making an overall profit after you've paid them.

Basically, there's no escaping from the admin, so you might as well embrace it and be good at it. And a great way of learning it is a job in admin while you work on your dream. Unless your dream is to work in admin, in which case I salute you and I wish you the dreamiest filing system known to man.

People can do more than one thing, and it's never too late to change your mind. One of my heroes is national treasure Julie Walters and before she became an actor, she was a trained nurse. Large-collared comedian Harry Hill used to be a doctor. Physics professor and science presenter Brian Cox used to be a rock star. Chat show host Ellen Degeneres was a paralegal in a law firm. Lifestyle guru Martha Stewart, famous for her home-making skills, was formerly a stockbroker. Pope Francis worked in a chemistry lab. And Judi Dench . . . well, Judi Dench was always an actor; she's Judi Dench.

There is no elusive 'right path'. There are just great paths, loads of them – all different and any number of them could be right for you, whether it's the path of enlightenment, the corporate ladder or the yellow brick road. Any number of them could be even better than what you have 'dreamed of'.

Not just career wise. In your personal life – you can't tell what's round the corner. You might live alone, have four flatmates, a partner or live with ten dogs who you love more than you love people. You might be straight, gay, trans or not know yet. You might change, you might find out things about yourself or just fall in love with someone who doesn't fit what you expected. You might want kids, you might decide you don't want kids or you might end up with eleven of them. You might be single or in a thruple; you might marry just at the point you'd given up on it and get two teenage step-kids you never saw coming and spend your weekends playing *Mario Party* and watching *Big Mouth* on Netflix. Don't pin yourself down too early.

And if you don't end up doing what you expected, that might be awesome. It might be better. You might become a ballet-dancing welder, a professional ice-cream taster or the person who develops an app that identifies which film or actor your mum is describing-in-an-incredibly-vague-way.

Don't put the blinkers on and race towards that one fixed point you've got in your head. Take the blinkers off. Look around you. You don't know all your options yet.

Don't follow your dreams. Just keep rewriting them.

Don't let your abs be bigger than your personality

I suppose I must have abs. But I've no real evidence that I do. Every so often, I suspect I've spotted one and it turns out to be a rib. Mostly, I think 'abs' are a fictional thing – a myth perpetrated by gym adverts, makers of superhero costumes and the people behind *Love Island*. I've never seen an ab in real life, only ever on TV. I have met Mark Wright *and* David Haye, but they were both wearing shirts so did nothing to dispel the idea that 'Abs' is a fantastical idea dreamt up by the manager of the 90s boyband 5ive who needed a fifth personality type for the final member and was struggling for inspiration.

I hate exercise. It's easy to say, I know, and it's often said but I really mean it.

'But Rachel, haven't there been times when you've felt really happy and exhilarated after running around on a sunny day or finishing a really hard work out?'

Yes, of course, there have been those occasions and I can count them on one hand. I've tried different exercises. I've done yoga and pilates; I've joined various gyms and aerobics sessions. I have tried many sports briefly, but I've got terrible co-ordination so anything involving hitting a ball is a total waste of time – football, cricket, tennis, hockey, rounders, squash, golf, badminton, netball, basketball – for me these are exercises in missing the ball and going to retrieve the ball I missed like a sad dog. In recent years I have been lucky enough to have a personal trainer. They've been brilliant and when I'm doing the work with them, I can manage to get all fit and strong which feels awesome. But the actual exercise, in spite of their fantastic efforts for variety and fun and enjoyment, is still exercise. A good personal trainer, in my opinion, is good at their job if they're able to persuade someone like me to exercise in spite of my continuing to hate exercise. And that's what personal trainers are for, and that's why so many rich people are thin: long-term physical coercion.

To be honest, when people talk about the feeling of happiness they get after a hard workout I suspect what they are describing is a mixture of smugness and relief that it's over. Runners are especially fond of this: 'Running makes me feel so *alive*', they say, which is funny because running makes me feel Dead.

'But what about endorphins?'

YEAH ALRIGHT, it releases endorphins, fine. So yes, okay, exercise is good for your mental health, of course, and yes, you can get a nice warm chemical glow from getting all sweaty and knackered, but you can get a nice warm glow from loads of things: curry, a log fire, snogging – all infinitely preferable to exercise.

I'm being churlish and I'm not actually advocating *not exercising*. I do recommend exercising. I recommend doing loads of things I don't like. Brushing your teeth isn't **fun** but you should certainly do it; that's not something you should compromise on. You can't just have a Smint and hope for the best. I'm just saying that exercise, for some people, it's never going to be enjoyable no matter how hard you try. No matter how calming yoga is, or how inventive a new weights machine is at the gym or how fresh the air feels on my face when I run, there is no getting away from it – I really really love sitting on my arse, and I always will.

Fitness is a useful thing to have in life but being fit doesn't necessarily mean you're happy. You can be physically fit and still miserable. You can be physically fit and an awful person. You can be buff and unhealthy, thin but unwell. Exercise can contribute to your misery – people can exercise to blot out problems or because they feel insecure, and people can over-exercise just as easily as they can overeat. You can become addicted to exercise. I've seen it happen and it is as horrible to watch as any addiction spiralling out of control. But less easy to help because of the idea that exercise is always good for you.

So, in saying 'Don't let your abs be bigger than your personality', I guess the writer's point is that exercise by itself isn't enough to make you happy. It's generally a positive thing, obviously. Whether it's walking your labradoodle or sweaty dancing in nightclubs or discovering Tough Mudder as you hit your fifties, there is lots of good to be had by moving around. Exercise changes some people's lives for the better and doing some exercise is much better than doing no exercise. All I'm saying is, even if exercise is your career and your passion, there are more important things than abs (your pelvic floor, for example – believe me, THAT is worth working at) and that for some people, exercise will always be a pain in the [flabby, happy] arse.

When in doubt, wing it

I would hate to come across as biased or partisan in any way so when I say that the last few years of politics in the UK have been a chronic shit-show of incompetent, desperate, clueless guesswork at best, and deliberate and corrupt sabotage at worst, I can only hope that is taken in a spirit of complete neutrality.

In the words of Theresa May, let me be very clear: Winging It is a perfectly acceptable strategy for making a sandwich, wrapping an oddly shaped gift or arguably, writing a book. No-one's life is ruined if you hate this paragraph. Winging It is not an acceptable strategy for governing a country. Winging It is not *best practice* for a negotiation with the EU that landed the economy in deep shit, and Winging It is far from ideal when the country finds itself overtaken by a worldwide pandemic and you haven't got time to attend the Cobra meetings about it cos you're, I don't know, having one of those really nice long showers or back-combing your thatched hair on five different occasions. If you're running the country, and you're in doubt, 'winging it' shouldn't be the answer. But that's exactly what's been happening in the last few years of this Tory government.

But it is hardly surprising given who keeps being elected.

Since Alexander Boris De Pfeffel Johnson was elected on the intelligent and nuanced party message of Let's Biff On and Get Brexit Done Chaps, it's been a steep decline into baseline incompetency and moral turpitude, yes turpitude. And he's roped an entire cabinet into his mummers' farce. I say all this with no ill will towards him or his band of limply loyal wet wipes that he calls his cabinet. Just joshing, I bear them loads of ill will, the way anyone would bear ill will towards people who hurt your country, hurt the poor, hurt children and reward their already loaded pals with billions of pounds from taxpayer money to do vital, potentially lifesaving, jobs to a level of incompetency so high it could wave at Elon Musk in space. Ill will doesn't go far enough. I wish them self-awareness or the Bubonic Plague, whichever would be worse. I hope very much that by the time this book is published, somehow an emergency general election has happened, provoked by Boris shock-resigning and initially running off with an enlivened Prue Leith and then going to jail, and a newly healed and robust Labour party, led by an emboldened Chris Packham, running on a campaign of fairness and badgers, who is dealing sensibly and calmly with the consequences of a dramatic Reverse-Brexit, and governing a country that feels united in its attitudes to Europe, poverty, refugees, anti-semitism, Black Lives mattering, whether 'MeToo' has gone too far actually and the length of Amanda Holden's dresses on *BGT*. I hope so, but I doubt it. We have a few years more in this mire so let's get our wellies on and start kicking.

People who've gone to public schools like Eton know how to wing it and generally they're good at it. A kid at any private school (I was one) is told 'well, yes, of course you can' as a general theme – can I learn Spanish instead of French? Yes! Can I start up a lunchtime drama club in my spare time? Yes, go ahead! Can I write a comedy song about our headmistress to the tune of YMCA with a choreographed dance and perform it at her final assembly before she leaves? Yes, go for it, Parris! [Of COURSE, this actually happened.] Take a school like Eton, and you multiply that privilege by a factor of, I don't know, the number of swans that dwell on their front lawn. So, when an Etonian politician becomes PM, one who at Eton was described as having a 'disgracefully cavalier attitude', they wing it. But crucially they don't even know that's what they're doing – they think the low-level haphazard actions they're taking, held together with handshakes, bluster and crossed fingers are actually them doing their job. Just as Boris' school report says he was 'surprised not to be appointed

NEVER PASS UP
THE OPPRTUNITY
FOR A WEE .

DON'T WORRY
ABOUT THE
THINGS YOU
CAN'T CHANGE
ANYWAY

Marry a
Plumber!
(they'll fix your pipes!)

TELL HER YOU
LOVE HER AND
NEVER BUY A
SECOND HAND
WET SUIT.

Don't a waste a
hot second
trying to fold
a fitted sheet.

(You're Welcome)

Don't worry about
things you
can't control.

What's for
you won't
pass you!

Don't
be a
DICK

Wake up.
Kich Ass.
Be Kind.
Repeat!!

Check your jeans
have _actual_ pockets
before you buy them
- not stupid fake
pockets for women
with invisible stuff

Always rinse your
weetabix / porridge bowl
out straight away - before
it turns to concrete.

You can never have
enough tampons....
Stuff them everywhere!

Don't let your abs
be bigger than
your personality.

whatever you
do ... do NOT
sleep with ▓▓▓
either of them.

Don't go in the
loft when
you're pissed

NAP WHENEVER
YOU CAN .

Smile as much

as possible

STAY
HYDRATED
(+ RESPECT
WOMEN)

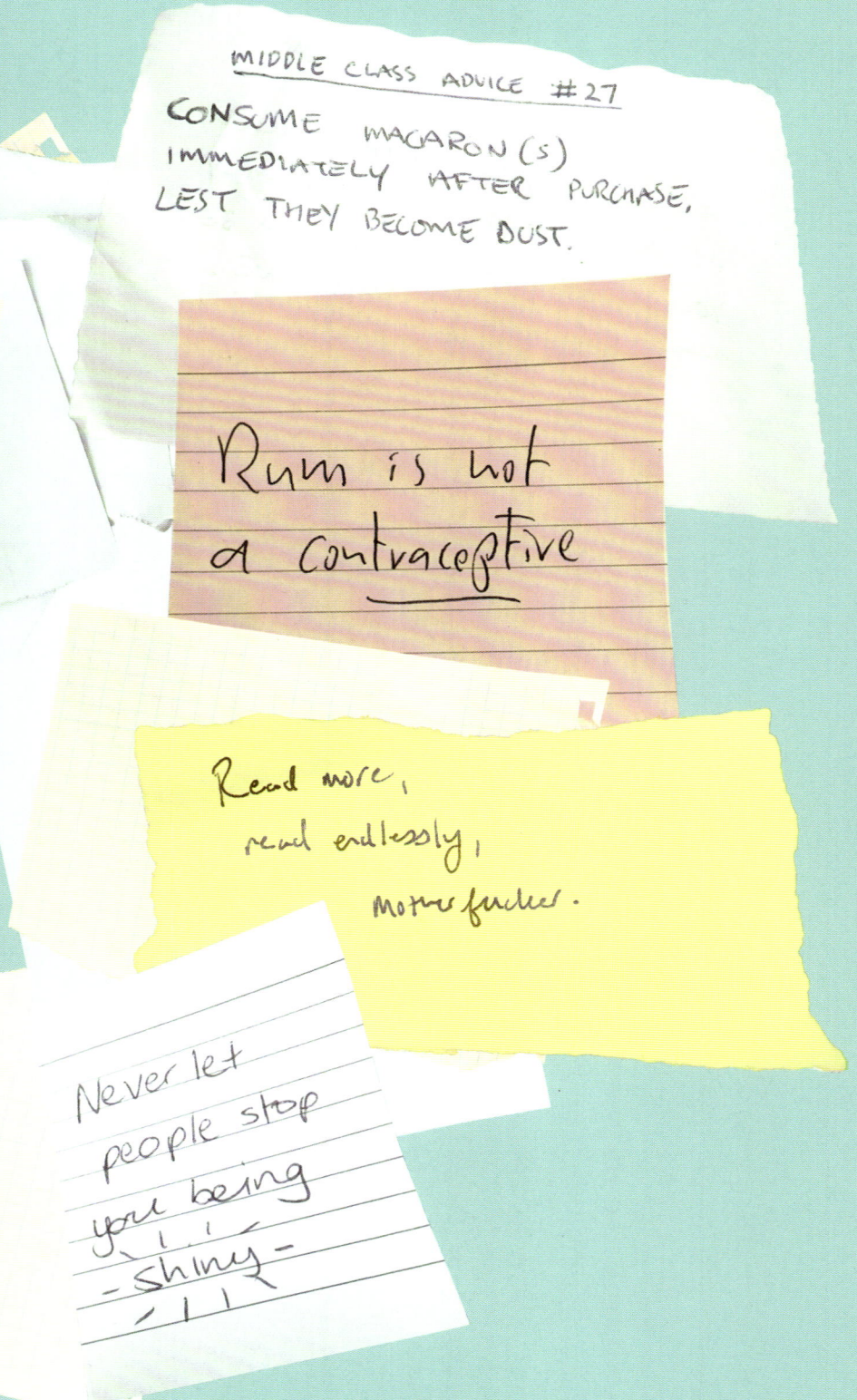

MIDDLE CLASS ADVICE #27

CONSUME MACARON(S) IMMEDIATELY AFTER PURCHASE, LEST THEY BECOME DUST.

Rum is not a contraceptive

Read more,
read endlessly,
motherfucker.

Never let
people stop
you being
- shiny -

When in doubt
– wing it.

You c...
well
reason
† †?

If you know
you're bad at
carrying drinks,
don.t try to be
the big man. You'll spill

Al...
a...
co...
Can...

Always follow your
dreams, unless
it is one of those
weird dreams
where you are
having sex with
your boss with
your partner watching

...out
...ol.
...lts

...anything you like
...life — within
...men, don't
...Pope, obviously

Don't sleep
with the
bassist.

...ys bring
...en
...wo)

...bingo dabber)

SINCERITY IS THE KEY,
YOU HAVE TO BE ABLE TO
FAKE SINCERITY.

All you need to
remember
Phone, wallet, keys

EVEN A SMALL
PEICE OF CARD
CAN MAKE YOU
FEEL INCLUDED
- SMALL THINGS MATTOE

Travel lot. If things go wrong.
Don't give another day. Don't
worry too much.

Always

Don't get
anyones name
tattooed on
yourself

Always pee after
sex

It'll probably
be fine if
you just
have another
few minutes
lie - in.

A cup of tea really
does make things
better

When life closes one
door, open it again!
It's a door thats
how they fucking work

Captain of the School',[21] he clearly expects to find himself in extraordinarily high positions in spite of his abilities. He supposes perhaps, he is Prime Minister because he deserves to be, rather than it being a terrible consequence of a broken system, the desperate votes of a disenfranchised country sold a pack of lies and an apparent national desire to be led by those who would once have been our feudal overlords, no matter how much stupider than us they may be.

My husband and I have different experiences of private school. He went to several, having been expelled from three. Although intelligent, he was not a high achiever at school or given particular encouragement, and yet, he still emerged from his education with a sense of 'I can probably do that'. That sense is what led him to booking a canal boating holiday and being absolutely convinced he knew how to drive a barge without so much as a desultory google.

Me, on the other hand – I went to an independent school, but only thanks to an assisted place, and so have the confidence of a privately schooled person mixed with the imposter-syndrome self-doubt of a scholarship girl. My psyche is all 'I *can't* do this . . . but I know that better than *anyone*!'

It is also a class difference – if you have access to opportunities, money, connections, then everything seems possible, or even, relatively easy. And you carry that into your work. So, say you're tasked with urgently co-ordinating a national response to growing mortalities, set against terrible economic implications, which is a hard task, instead of realising how hard it is, you wing it – you ask for favours off neighbours, you get people to clap, you blame 'mutant algorithms', you dissemble and fake until it's over and when the rest of the world notices our national response was deadly and abysmal, you just chant 'world-beating vaccination programme' at the camera until you pass out.

The way I feel about the Conservative government of the last few years is that there have been daily reminders that we are, as the saying goes, being led by donkeys, except the donkeys are the donkeys who the donkey man can't use anymore because they can't even stand up straight, they keep walking into the pier and aren't very nice to small children. Every senior minister appears less intelligent, less honest, less competent and definitely less compassionate than nearly anyone else I know, and I know some awful people.

Take Failing Chris Grayling's £89 million ferry contract to a company with no ferries or Gavin Williamson's 'mutant algorithm' depriving a generation of meaningful A-level results or Matt Hancock's dangerous liasons. As Home Secretary, Priti Patel didn't know what counterterrorism was. As Brexit Secretary, Dominic Raab didn't know Dover was important to UK trade. Brexit has already been a disaster – from a fuel crisis to a mass cull of thousands of pigs – and the best response from our Prime Minister was him repeatedly shouting 'Have you ever had a bacon sandwich?!' at Andrew Marr.

They don't know what they're doing, they've made catastrophic, deadly mistakes, and there have been scant resignations. Yes, scant. There have been almost no consequences for a group of politicians who have been winging it through an international pandemic and a historical re-ordering of Nations. They should know *more* than us. They should be *better* at this than us. We ought to have higher expectations than we currently do. We shouldn't be making bargains with them like, 'Well, they voted not to feed the poorest children in society, but to be fair, they haven't yet brought back the death penalty* so today is a good day.' Or, 'Well, well, Boris may have illegally siphoned off jobs and money to someone he was sleeping with while he was London Mayor, but he did make me laugh on that zip line hahaha.' We have all made political mistakes but voting in Johnson and his cabinet of cronies was one of our biggest. Please don't do this again. If it looks like an unthinking and arrogant millionaire playboy

---

* Priti Patel is in favour of the death penalty. No surprises really.

incapable of serious thought and it smells like an unthinking and arrogant millionaire playboy incapable of serious thought, it probably is one.

I believe, from what I've seen and people I have known, that one of the hallmarks of an upper-class education and upbringing is a certain intellectual bravado – an unquestioning self-confidence that the very privileged have from birth, no matter how dim they are, and less privileged people do not inherit, no matter how well educated they are. It seems to manifest as an understanding that basically, without much evidence to back it up, you are probably correct most of the time. And it often comes with a voice to carry over the heads of poorer people. It is a lesson in blagging, in pushing things through, in winging it. Boris has been winging it all this time. The problem is, he isn't actually any good at it.

He has led his loyal brigade of low-intelligence, low-morality cronies through one of the most dangerous times in British history, from the medical threat of the virus to the economic threat of lockdowns and the alarming but entirely predictable repercussions of Brexit. It would have been difficult for any leader; it was a perilously difficult task. But in selecting for his cabinet only politicians loyal to him, loyal to Brexit and with no other discernible skills and refusing to sack them or punish them following their many disasters, he let the country down in the worst way possible. 'Winging It' is a fun turn of phrase when applied to botching a recipe, fixing a wonky table or blagging your way through a Geography GCSE. But when you're winging it with people lives, it's time to stop doing what you're doing, say sorry, and step away.

Don't be a dick

We're all a dick. You can't *not* be a dick 100% of the time, therefore – yes, I've done the maths – you are going to be a dick some of the time. Some of the biggest dicks are the ones who think they're never a dick and they can tell you not to be a dick when they're being a dick actually. Also, dicks are subjective – someone might think you're being a dick and maybe you don't think you are being a dick, and there's really no way of deciding for sure without an outside adjudicator, and they might not know either – look at Solomon and that baby. What a dick.

So, you know, try not to be *too* much of a dick, all of the time. You don't want your epitaph to read 'Mostly a dick'. But equally, we all find ourselves sometimes in a state of dickishness at one time or another. Such is the way of the dick.

The only thing to fear is fear itself

This bit of stirring advice came via an audience member but is from President Roosevelt's inauguration speech in 1933: 'Let me assert my firm belief that the only thing we have to fear is . . . fear itself.' It's a great quotation and offers a lot to think about.

Firstly, it's not true. There's loads to fear, at any time.

Here are some things to fear apart from fear itself:

Getting nits
The rise of the Far Right
Speaking in public
A worldwide pandemic
Losing your job
The Far Right giving you nits
Your children being secretly evil
Deep Vein Thrombosis
A drone flying into your head
Being cancelled
Becoming like your parents
Becoming like your children (possibly evil)
Cats
Forgetting how to write with a pen
That the helicopters you can hear over your house at night ARE there for you
Walking alone at night

Walking alone at night and bumping into the Far Right and them
giving you nits
Getting pregnant
Never getting pregnant
Falling off your bike
Criminals
The police
Getting pregnant by the Far Right
Salmonella
War

There are definitely real things to fear, so, ultimately, this quote is a
lie. But many things that can be good are based on lies: Father Christmas, surprise birthday parties, contouring, CGI, polite declines, faith
in a higher power, Rylan's face.

Let's think about what that speech was for. Bear in mind Roosevelt
came into power at the peak of the Great Depression. Unemployment
in the USA was at 25% – 12 million Americans were jobless, industry
was simply shutting down and crop prices had sunk by 60%. In addition, though Roosevelt wasn't to know this then, a severe drought
– the 'Dust Bowl' – swept the heartlands of America in the mid to late
thirties and hot on the heels of that, came World War Two. In short,
the country Roosevelt addressed had much to fear – real, palpable,
life-threatening problems – hunger, homelessness, hopelessness. The
Depression had begun in 1929, so it wasn't new, and it wasn't going
away quickly. Many of the American people (and people all over the
world) were desperate and afraid and ready to give up.

So, as he took to that podium, he needed to rally his people. The
address he gave was similar to a battle speech. It was partly strategy:
much of the speech was Roosevelt laying out a very specific policy
plan to show people how they, as a country, would fight this. But as

in any great battle speech, he also needed to uplift them, to inspire them. He continued on from the quote above by describing this fear, this 'unjustified terror, which paralyses needed efforts to convert retreat into advance'. This is the language of war – the need for advance, not retreat.

Fear can be debilitating and can make your situation worse. When I had a mental breakdown, what drove it, after the initial crash, was this terrible, overwhelming fear of it happening again, a fear of feeling as bad as I did before. That fear was what drove my anxiety, and the anxiety was the problem in and of itself. I suffered from fear of fear itself and it was crippling and I know I'm not alone. Fear when it takes over your life is paralysing.

Great speeches in history, and in literature and screenplays, have used fear as a tool to inspire people, but in different ways. In the St Crispin's Day Speech from Shakespeare's *Henry V*, Henry doesn't deny that there's anything to fear in the forthcoming battle but places honour and prestige and pride as balancing factors in whether they stay to fight. It's a great character decision for Henry to not force or cajole his frightened men into battle. He suggests that those who are afraid, should leave, and that's okay, and there will be no repercussions for them:

'. . . he which hath no stomach to this fight,
Let him depart; his passport shall be made
And crowns for convoy put into his purse:
We would not die in that man's company
That fears his fellowship to die with us.'

But he makes that sound like a sad option for them that they will regret; that the lucky ones are the ones who stay. Sure, it's going to be a bloody battle, but Henry manages to convince us that the greater thing to fear is missing out this last great hurrah!* Henry is essentially wielding FOMO as a battle cry.

In 1585, Elizabeth I made a speech to her troops going into the Spanish Armada. She said 'Let tyrants fear' – making fear a thing only villains experience. She went on to say her lack of fear came from her faith in her people: '. . . under God, I have placed my chiefest strength and safeguard in the loyal hearts and good-will of my subjects.' She inspired her troops by saying: YOU are the reason I'm not afraid. Who could desert her then?

Both she and Shakespeare use the stomach to talk about being afraid: 'I may have the body of a weak and feeble woman, but I have the heart and stomach of a king,' she says, assuring her soldiers that if she, a woman, can hold no fear in her gut, then what are they, if they do? Misguided gender perceptions aside, it's a good tactic.

George VI addressed the UK as we joined World War Two – on the radio. He used fear in a different way again. He said that without our country taking this action, others would live in 'the bondage of fear'. He laid the hopes of vulnerable others at our door; he implied it was up to us to defend those who are afraid.

All these great and undoubtedly inspiring speeches, find a way of side-stepping fear, of persuading people to forget it or ignore it or that they shouldn't feel it in the first place. But fear is not always unhealthy. Appropriate fear makes us better at looking after people, looking after the environment, looking after ourselves. Necessary fear guides our decisions. We look twice while crossing the road and we wear seatbelts in cars, but we also go on rollercoasters and go out without sunscreen on and take our brakes off going downhill on a bicycle and shout 'weeeeee'.

---

* Worth noting that while 'Freedoooooom' was the takeaway from that fictional William Wallace battle scene in *Braveheart*, that speech used the same tactics as Shakespeare's *Henry V* – compare a blue-faced Mel Gibson saying 'And dying in your beds many years from now, would you be willing to trade all the days from this day to that for one chance, just one chance to come back here?' with 'Old men forget . . . but he'll remember with advantages what feats he did that day . . . And gentlemen in England now a-bed, shall think themselves accursed they were not here.'

Across the world we have been united in the last few years by a common fear: fear of disease, death and bereavement. Fear of being trapped inside, fear of losing our way of life, fear of losing our livelihoods. That universal fear is never welcome but actually, it can bind people together and it's not in itself always bad. We need some fear in our lives, and just because we fear something, it doesn't mean we won't embrace it. You can want something badly even if it scares you. A lot of my life falls into this category – moving to London, attempting an uncertain career, doing standup, being in the public eye, becoming a step-mum, getting pregnant, becoming a mother; these things terrified me, and they were, and are, as scary now, but I still want them and I still do them.

I wonder what inspiring speeches look like if they acknowledge that everyone is absolutely terrified? It's still very rare. In President Biden's speech of 11th March 2021, which came exactly one year after the first Covid shutdown, he said emphatically, 'I will tell you the truth'. He compared the situation to a war, he said 'this isn't over' he said there was a long way to go. He was honest but he didn't talk about fear.

Whereas Jacinda Ardern, the president of New Zealand, acknowledged it straight away in her speech at the start of the Covid crisis in 2020. She says, within the first minute, 'I understand that all this rapid change creates anxiety and uncertainty'. She has her rousing inspiring lines, but they are a different tone to the speeches of most of her counterparts. 'We may not have experienced anything like this in our lifetimes, but we know how to rally and we know how to look after each other, and what could be more important than that? So, for now, please, be strong, be kind and unite.'[22] It's less about not being scared and more about caring for each other. I can't help but think Ardern being a woman has some bearing on those differences in rhetoric and that that take is something new and something needed.* The majority

---

* Indeed, countries with female leadership were shown to have handled Covid better than those under male leadership, with earlier lockdowns and fewer deaths.

of rhetoric around comforting people is saying: do not be afraid, there is nothing to fear. But as a society I think we are learning that it's okay to be afraid. Inspiring, rallying speeches on the cusp of war or hardship or the unknown, can be rousing and strong but still truthful.

What would those historical speeches look like if the leaders admitted that they, and their followers, were afraid?

Here is my re-telling of that Henry V speech but a little less dignified and a little more honest:

Writers note: please perform in full-throated RADA-trained classical voice, with appropriate blocking. And in armour.

I ask you now, my brothers, for I say
That he who fights and sheds his blood this day;
He *is* my brother! and I now beseech;
Who here in line is fearful of this breech?

This battle, where the other troops amount
To nigh 12 thousand at the highest count.
And we, just nine. Nine guys?! Doesn't look great . . .
And yet, with such men, who could be afraid?

I am. I am . . . afraid? I must say aye.
My pants are wetter than fresh April's dew
My stones have shrunk away all up inside –
Right up there, gone, my manhood with them too.

I'm shaking in my boots, and rivulets
Of wee are flowing, streaming, down my thighs.
I've got the willies, I am wigging out,
I'm sweating everywhere, e'en from my eyes.

Am I afraid, me with this crappy sword,
A sword so small, not fit for King nor foe?
Do I wish for a larger sword? Hell yes!
But could I carry such a one, when, lo!

My hands are shaking like a stupid leaf;
My psoriasis is playing up, such tricks!
And yet in truth, I'd hold my manhood cheap
if I did not admit to shitting bricks.

And so my point, I guess, is that we ALL
Are doomed, I mean, we do not stand a chance.
But we should *probably* plough on, with gall –
And face down those 12 thousand pricks from France

Because if by some teensy tiny ray
Of hope, or by the blessing of God's hand,
We somehow, somehow make it through this day
And gain this arid, scrubby patch of land –

Then, we'll look really good. Think on't my men –
If we do this all by ourselves and win,
We're legends to the ladyfolk, my friends,
We'll be as God, but sexier than him.

And so, with honour and with withered plums,
I say to you: Go forward into this fight.
And forevermore they'll say of Henry's sons:
They pissed themselves but did not pause to wipe.

Marry a plumber! (They'll fix your pipes!)

Hands up, I'll be the first to admit, I haven't married a plumber. My bad. I dropped the ball*cock* there but hopefully I've now *piped* up just in time for you to amend your *coupling* plans, and before *u-bend* the knee, you can *solder* on and find a person who *valve*-ues you, and who knows their way around your… *flange*.

Okay enough of that, but I like what this advice gets to, at the heart of it. I know it's a joke but it has some truth to it and that truth is: it's no bad thing to make a practical choice in a partner. (Not too practical or literally everyone would be gunning for Jay Blades from the *Repair Shop*, and he's got enough on his hands.) It's an old-fashioned idea in a sense, but then so are crumpets and I like them too.

I married someone who I fell head over heels in love with. But that doesn't mean there were absolutely no considerations apart from that fizzy-feeling-at-the-bottom-of-your-stomach. Don't get married based on that – after all it might turn out to be a stomach ulcer, and a shot of Pepto-Bismol on the honeymoon might cause you to start having regrets.

I got together with my husband when I was 33 and he was 44. He was a divorcee with two children, and I had had my fair share of relationships before him. We had known each other as friends for quite a few years before it became romantic, and I believe we finally got together at a time when we'd both worked out what it was we wanted and needed and what we were capable of.

It is very possible to be a giddy romantic, and deeply in love, without believing in notions such as 'The One'. I don't believe in 'The

One'. I barely believe in *The One Show*. I don't believe in destiny, or One True Love or Soulmates. The stats of there being one person in the world meant for you, regardless of language, culture or proximity means that the concept of soulmates is actually quite a bleak one. What are the chances of you finding your soulmate if they happen to be a Brazilian miner, and you don't have the income to pay for long haul flights? What if 'The One' is Justin Trudeau, and unfortunately, he's already married and has never even visited your home in Burton Upon Trent? Maybe your One True love is charming, gorgeous and single but is serving 13 years for armed robbery? Hardly anyone would ever meet their soulmate if there was just one person out there for you. And popular phrases like 'hopelessly in love' or 'helplessly in love' suggest you are entirely passive in it, which I don't buy. I think it's actually more romantic to think that we choose, that it isn't decided for us. I think there are quite a few people out there for each person and who you choose dictates the kind of life you live and the kind of person you become. I would have become a different version of me if I'd stayed with either of my previous partners. Not better or worse, but different, and probably vegan.

I believe someone you love can *become* 'The One', through years of love, patience, shared experience, trust, as well as strict training, a list of rules and a lot of post-it notes stuck to the fridge.

There are different kinds of love, and I think for first-dates love to become long-term love, there are certain things you need to share, on top of butterflies, great sex and making each other laugh.

Here's what I think they are:

First of all, you need a spark. Whether it's physical or intellectual or high quality bantz or you just can't stop finishing each other's sentences – you should light each other up.

Next, shared goals. This sounds very serious to be second on the list but IMHO you might as well figure this out early on, if you really like someone and want to spend more than, say, a few weeks tangled in their 10-tog. Now, I'm approaching this from the point of view of dating between about 25 and 50; these questions might be different if you're outside those, but to be honest if you're a fresh-faced 18-year-old, don't go looking for a life partner yet – have some fun! Make some awful sticky mistakes! And if you're over 65, I verrry much doubt you're taking the relationship advice of a 37-year-old comedian. So, IF you're in a situation where you have some specific life plans, it's useful to ask some questions early on.

Here is a list of big hitters that might be handy:

- Do you want to have children ever?
- Is your career one you're passionate about or is it just a job to you?
- Do you have plans to travel the world?
- When do you want to have children?
- What's your relationship with your family?
- How many children do you want?
- When can we start trying?
- What do you do again?
- What paternity leave do they offer?

Your questions might be different obviously.

But in all seriousness, that kids one is a fundamental one for many people and worth finding out sooner rather than later – whether you are on the 'yes, please, five by the time I'm 30!' end of the spectrum or more on the 'yikes, no brats, thank you, triple condoms til I die' end. But for others, travel, lifestyle, income, location, religion or an intolerance to wheat are factors that could make or break a relationship.

Here are some important revelations THE BIG QUESTIONS *could* throw up:

She wants to have children and, necessarily, quite soon
They don't want children
Her dogs are her children
He already has seven children, who are all strong singers, respond to a whistle and live in a mansion in Salzburg
She's actually been on sabbatical while you've been dating but ordinarily works 70 hours a week minimum
They hate their job and are very protective of time outside work
He really thinks of himself as a writer . . .
They have plans to quit their job next week and live in Indonesia for a year
He spends half his year in Salzburg with his seven children
She really loves taking ketamine
He has a huge, close-knit family who take up a lot of his time and they already want to meet you
She does not have any family; the only family she has known were the nuns in the convent in Salzburg
They don't believe in monogamy
He wants to get married in the next year
She is teetotal
He is a Real ale man
He's had a previous ten-year relationship but they never moved in together . . .
She's a millionaire, doesn't work, hates children, and is, to be specific, a Baroness, in Salzburg

These things can make or break a relationship, but that's not to say that if all the practicalities are in place, then the relationship will work. You can never predict falling out of love with someone, or in love with someone else, or simply not wanting to live in a certain life anymore. You might have the perfect set-up for what you thought you wanted and then wake up one morning at 46, take one look at your least favourite novelty tea towel (not suggesting that as a nickname for your partner) and feel an intractable urge to be single.

What we want from a partner changes as we get older, and it's not just that you start logically *wanting* someone that can fix a plug, but actually *fancying* someone who can. I used to find things like mysteriousness and inner demons and an unruly thick head of hair, sexy. As I have gotten older, I've found other things sexy: emotional strength, steadfastness, fatherhood, male pattern baldness. (I jest.) (Partly.)

On *The Mash Report* a few years ago, comedian Geoff Norcott did a bit that I mostly agree with – and that's why it stands out in my head. Discussing toxic masculinity, host Nish Kumar asked him: 'Don't you think that heterosexual women want emotionally intuitive men rather than a return to, sort of, unreconstructed manliness?' to which Geoff replied: 'No, they want *both* . . . Some of them might want, y'know, a bloke to read poetry, but, equally, there are a lot of women who want their fella to stop crying and bleed the fucking radiator; let's be honest.'

. . . which was greeted with whoops and cheers from the live audience – the progressive, left-wing, feminist audience. Everyone, not least Geoff, was a bit surprised by the reaction. What I think I, and possibly a lot of that audience would add, is that it needn't be gendered. Most people, once they reach a certain age, want a partner who doesn't just sit around being willfully enigmatic or constantly hilarious or just an absolute pleasure to behold. We want a partner who has the capacity to deal with difficult things, who is useful, self-motivating and who can support us practically through life. That doesn't necessarily mean they can definitely rewire a plug but someone who brings something to the table in everyday life: someone who can offer advice, comfort, ideas, enthusiasm, experience, the ability to remember dates, arrange hang-outs with friends and know what needs getting from the shop. Basically, sharing the load, one way or another.

My love for my husband, even in the few years we've been together, has changed and grown. When we got together, we had the spark and the butterflies and all that and we still do but now there's more. We make each other laugh, all the time, we have worked at making a blended family together, we have private family jokes and 'bits' between us and the kids that no-one else gets and *that* special car dance we all do to 'Walk Of Life' by Dire Straits. In our first two years of marriage, he and I have shared all of lockdown, our careers and incomes disappearing, trying for a baby, pregnancy, loss, grief . . . all of which has bonded us more than anything before. Neither of us could have predicted when we got together what the other was capable of when it came to the things we have been through in these past two years. There have been some very dark times, and I think we both felt lucky to have somehow stumbled upon a partner who was able to cope, to carry on, but also emotional enough to support the other, to cry, to mourn together and to hold it all, indefinitely, as a part of our own special history. But I think maybe we weren't lucky. I think we chose well. I think a part of us did know what we were looking for, and searched, and found it.

You don't have to marry a plumber. You don't even have to marry someone Corgi-registered. But if you are making a choice in love, choose actively, not passively. Find yourself someone who can handle emotional stuff and real life. Choose to love someone who adds to your life and you add to theirs. Choose a partner, not just a lover. Choose someone with the potential to become your 'The One'. And if they can fix your pipes as well, then, all to the good.

What's for you won't pass you #2

25 June 2021

I write this at 34 weeks pregnant with my second pregnancy. He is kicking as I write, and I feel glad every day that my son is such a lairy baby, even when he's settled on my bladder and seems to enjoy Irish dancing. I love the reassurance. It makes me feel hopeful that in a few weeks, I will have a baby. Hopeful but not certain.

In the last month I've been out and about more with bits of work, meeting people who don't know me and when people see my bump, they ask 'Is it your first?' I've been asked that question about four times a day on any working day and it's always meant well, but I'm not sure what to tell them. Because, at present, he is not my first anything. He is the second baby I've carried; he has been in my belly for a few weeks longer than my daughter was, but at present, I have had two pregnancies and no children. But it's a question asked quickly, in passing, by kindly strangers, who aren't expecting a long answer, and so I've said 'yes' quite often, and it hasn't really felt true, and it isn't.

'*Will* he be your first child?' might be easier to answer, that slight change in phrasing marking an understanding that I don't yet have a child, not in the sense most people mean, but it's a huge, terrifying question in itself, when you think about it. The answer being, I mean, I really hope so, yes, but who knows? I hope he goes on to be my first child. The certainty of other mothers still shocks me – pregnant women who talk openly in early months with an absolute surety that they will have a baby at a given time at a given month. That, I'm sure, is a better way to be, and I am jealous of their certainty, but I also feel

191

scared for them, protective of them and find myself praying for them – to someone, not sure what or who. I am grateful that I at least have hope now and more confidence in the pregnancy than I did up until a month ago. The day when I was told 'if he came now, he'd survive' was a huge relief; I had been holding my breath to get to that point.

I feel, in fact, so happy, so content, that it scares me. It feels too perfect. I am in love with my husband, we have a family and a house, and I am pregnant and it is summer and some days it feels so perfect, I'm scared something will go wrong like it did before. I hope when this book comes out, I have a baby boy. I feel I know him a bit already. His kicking and moving make me laugh – they're so strange and strong. I find him eccentric, a bit of a character, even now. The thought of losing him is so heartbreaking that I can hardly even think about it, but people do, don't they, so I do, think about it, I have to. My husband worries, I know, that I think too much about baby loss – that I am too aware of the statistics of late miscarriage, of stillbirth, but, when you have been that unlikely statistic, it is hard not to consider them again. My husband loves me and wants me to be free of that knowledge, for it not to spoil my pregnancy, I think. But it is a part of me now and a part of our journey, for both of us: a heightened awareness, a caveat, ears pricked up, ready for danger. I wonder if I will always be on the lookout, for the risks of loss, for how statistically likely a tragedy is. I wonder if I will always reach a point of happiness where it scares me, like a balloon floating so so high that it pops.

I'm glad that in the last few months I've felt more able to connect with my friends who gave birth around the time of our loss. It's taken a while, but more recently I've felt able to genuinely be happy and excited and supportive, I hope, albeit a little late. I thought it would be hard meeting their babies but, once I did, it was lovely because they were lovely, and – the truth was so obvious – this isn't my baby, it's theirs. There is nothing to fear here. It *was* hard seeing my husband playing with, and holding up, our baby nephew, very soon after the loss. That stung – he should be playing with our baby, I thought. This picture should have our baby in it, not that baby. He's holding someone else's baby; I haven't been able to give him a baby to hold. All that. It hurt. There will always be moments that sting but they are becoming less frequent.

It's nine months since we lost our first baby. I've been pregnant almost continuously for 15 months. I'm gagging for a glass of wine, my tits are unfathomably big – an unwieldy G cup – and, almost unbelievably, I'm really looking forward to doing some proper exercise. I first got pregnant a month into the first lockdown of 2020 and all being well, I'll be giving birth just as the UK is coming out of lockdown in 2021. This has been a very strange time, full of ups and downs and starts and ends, trials and gifts, and happiness and tragedy and so much love and care. I am already in love with my son, and I am bursting with excitement to meet him. People over-use the phrase 'I can't wait' but for me, it is a daily effort – I find it hard to concentrate; I count minutes and hours and days. I need him safe, where I can see him and hold him. I am hopeful. The sun took ages to come out this year – not like the balmy days of March last year – it has been a rainy, cold spring but the sun has finally come out in these early June days. I hope it stays until he arrives. I hope I am holding a hot, grumpy baby in the sweaty heat of August. I hope. I am happy, I am hopeful and I am grateful. I am ready.

Don't go in the loft when you're pissed

It was fun imagining what household incident provoked this advice, a drunken fall while putting Christmas decorations away? Dropping an open bottle of Baileys and it spilling stickily all over your daughter's childhood book collection? Getting locked in overnight without your phone, maybe falling asleep up there after a few gins in a tin? Perhaps attempting some risky DIY under the influence? I have images of an inebriated foot standing on a rusty nail, played out in a black-and-white slow-mo recreation at the start of 999 with Michael Buerk or a dramatic fall through the ceiling, as featured in one of the rare comic storylines of *Holby City*.

Or perhaps you shouldn't go in the loft when you're drunk because it might be even more scary than it already is. Attics are spooky places, unless you've turned yours into an ensuite double with multiple skylights. What might you find in your attic? A Jumanji board? A haunted oil painting that gets older and older? Hundreds of furious bloodthirsty birds? A chilling lack of loft insulation? Or, perhaps, ascending a darkened staircase, investigating the far-off screams and shouts you keep hearing in the night, you manage to navigate a series of locked doors into the attic, only to discover the horrifying spectacle of your lover's secret, mad, raging wife. This, after all, was the fate of Jane Eyre in Charlotte Brontë's Victorian classic, and I *do* like to think that after Jane Eyre had endured such a profoundly harrowing, horrifying, life-altering experience, that her takeaway lesson from it all would be, quite simply, 'Don't go in the loft when you're pissed'.

I first read *Jane Eyre* when I was 11. I've read it many more times between now and then. I could easily eulogise about how *vital a read it is for young women* but – well, I will, actually. *Jane Eyre* is a vital read for young women.

A strong female lead character, so far so good. She might not be covered in skintight latex 'armour' or be wearing a gold bikini or be able to sucker punch a mutant at short range but Jane Eyre is a stronger woman than many of the size eight botoxed honeys that grace our screens in Hollywood each year. They get given the moniker of 'strong female lead' because their stunt double does some excellent kickboxing in the fight scene. Meanwhile Jane is single-minded,* funny, resilient, stubborn, independent, irreverent,† well-educated but underprivileged. She's a feminist, before the word existed. 'Women are supposed to be calm generally, but women feel as much as men feel; they need exercise for their faculties, they suffer from too rigid a restraint, too absolute a stagnation precisely as men would suffer and it is narrow-minded . . . to say they ought to confine themselves to making puddings and knitting stockings. It is thoughtless to condemn them if they seek to do more, to learn more, than custom has pronounced necessary for their sex.' It's too big to fit on a T-shirt comfortably, but I'm saving up to get a full sleeve tattoo of that. Jane starts earning her own money the second she leaves school, she does not want to be dependent on any man, she is wilful and takes huge risks for the sake of living by her own rules. She refuses various offers of love or marriage because they do not meet her standards, either morally or romantically, and she's just generally a baller.

Then we have the fact that she isn't beautiful. Not at all. She's described, repeatedly, as '*plain*', which is 19th century speak for 'rough as old bags'. And it doesn't matter. Her story is as full of adventure, excitement, fear, love and, crucially, lust, as any of the Grade A

---

* I think Jane would have been a force to be reckoned with if she'd lived in the age of Twitter, with responses like 'I mentally shake hands with you for your answer, despite its inaccuracy'. ZING!

† When a sad, slightly self-pitying Rochester asks her 'Am I hideous, Jane?', she replies, 'Yes Sir. You always were, you know.' That's what you get for fishing.

Stunners that frequent the pages of other classic novels – Tess, Daisy, Lara, Anna, Estella, Catherine, Rebecca or Bathsheba, etc. Jane is plain, and it made no difference to her receiving two proposals of marriage and generous dollops of flirtation, romance and lust.

This was cheering for a young girl just embarking on adolescence, feeling fat and ugly and unattractive, to read. It was helpful for little me to learn that You Can Still Be Fancied Even If You Don't Look Like Natalie Imbruglia (this comparison was of its time). And if you think I should be saying 'you can still be *valued*' even if you're not beautiful – yes, sure, but that's different. I was lucky enough to feel valued in certain ways – valued as a hard worker, as a prefect (of course), as a sassy best friend, as a surprisingly good pool player, no matter what I looked like. But frankly what you're scared of when you're that age is never being *fancied* by anyone or anything, never finding the passionate, romantic love you read in books, unless you look a certain way. One of the less celebrated lessons I took from the novel was that witty, clever Jane Eyre was plain and still Rochester was crushing on her big time. Passionate Love and Lust don't just happen to people who make the FHM Sexiest Celebs list.

But enough of Jane. Let's talk about Bertha.

Things that go bump in the night have always fascinated us, from *A Christmas Carol* to *Most Haunted* with Yvette Fielding.* Brontë wielded this in the middle chapters of *Jane Eyre,* where Jane is essentially living in a haunted house with a vengeful spirit. It's like *The Haunting of Hill House* but with added lace and a large horse. It seems at times it's going to be your classic ghost story – the paranormal, mystical forces, standard spooksville. But she soon discovers it is not a spirit after all but ~~Yvette Fielding hiding in the wardrobe~~ the living, fuming wife of Mr Rochester, imprisoned in the attic.

---

* Of which, worth noting, there have been TWENTY-THREE series to date. It's been going on so long, Yvette is now close friends with several of the ghosts and they co-own a villa in the South of France. There's talk of a big reunion show with some of the ghosts from series one so fingers crossed for that.

His wife, Bertha, has been kept imprisoned there for years because she is, according to Rochester, insane and dangerous. She is referred to as 'it' and a 'figure'. She is dehumanised. She becomes a symbol of gothic horror, like Dracula or Frankenstein's monster. In fact, in the story, she is referred to as a 'goblin', a 'tigress', a 'vampire', even an 'unclothed hyena'.

But she is not a monster, she is a woman. So how has she come to hold as much fear and horror as any fictional demon?

The madwoman trope – from the vengeful Medea in Greek tragedy to Shakespeare's Ophelia* to rabbit-botherer Glenn Close in *Fatal Attraction* – is now a well-known one, but the truth is it has existed for thousands of years. It is used to entertain, to warn, to titillate and to control. The 'madwoman' is usually one or more of any of the things that freak out weak men – an angry woman, a powerful woman, a single woman, a sexual woman or a woman who won't smile for them.

Historically (as I imagine the average demographic of those reading this book already knows, you lovely feminist nerds), women have been labelled mad, insane, hysterical, unstable or emotional in order to reduce their power. Once someone is labelled as being hysterical or over-emotional, it is much easier to ignore, silence or undermine them. Once someone is labelled as crazy, it is much easier to remove them, kill them, burn them at the stake, lobotomise them,[†] or simply

---

* Ophelia, as an example of feminine madness, came in the 19th century to represent the most common form of female madness. Diagnoses of 'Ophelia syndrome' were widespread and described a feminine disposition towards hysteria and suicide, often after having been 'deflowered and abandoned'. So, basically, this form of madness described someone who had been mistreated and was consequently distressed. It was also, in serious psychological studies, as well as popular culture, conflated with women wearing their hair in a loose style. Kate Bush would stand no chance.

† In the 1940s to 70s in the UK and USA, women were disproportionately targeted for frontal lobotomies at the peak of this barbaric practice, particularly Black women. Women with depression or anxiety or 'agitated behaviour' (behaviour tolerated in male patients but not in female patients) were deemed good subjects for it. Many psychiatrists believed it was easier to return women, post-lobotomy, who had often lost all of their mental faculties and were therefore docile and quiet, to a life of domestic duties at home, than it was to rehabilitate lobotomised men back into a role as a wage earner.

imprison them – in an asylum, a jail or of course, your attic, or perhaps a high-spec loft conversion for the discerning mad wife.

That's the extreme end of it, but it's often much more subtle. The subsequent stigma takes power away from not just *that* woman, but *all* women: it furthers the idea that women are prone to a weak mental state; that we're the human equivalent of a water-balloon: fragile and floppy and quite fun if you handle it carefully but ultimately a bit silly and likely to explode at any moment if put under pressure. Calling women mad, or versions of it, happen every day in small ways that seem harmless but are evocative of something bigger. It's 'calm down' when you're already calm, 'someone's in a bad mood' when you're being assertive or 'stop panicking' when you steadily point out that your colleague's beefed-up Land Rover isn't going to fit under that height barrier he's careering towards. It's also impossible to defend against once it's out there. If someone says you're being over-emotional, it makes you emotional. If someone says 'you're getting angry' when you weren't, that is infuriating and you get angry in response. And if someone says you're mad, there is almost no way of responding that doesn't somehow confirm it. It's a brilliant, dangerous tool. When a woman steps out of line, there's a spectrum of ways to make her seem irrational. They're not always deployed consciously, with a devious sexist plan, but often come from a lack of understanding. But they make an impact, and it works.

During his presidency, Donald Trump was great at this tactic, amazing at it – he was the very best actually, the greatest at it in all of the world. He called Vice-President Kamala Harris 'a madwoman' and 'a monster'. He also said, during the Brett Kavanaugh hearings, '[Kamala] was the angriest of the group' playing on not only the over-emotional woman stereotype, but the angry Black woman stereotype (remember this was an attempted rape accusation against a man who would go on to wield the highest judicial power in the country). He's called Speaker Nancy Pelosi 'stone cold crazy' and told Greta Thunberg to 'chill'. He isn't a smart man, he's barely a legitimate human, but he knew the best way to appeal to his fanbase, and sexist and racist slurs are always going to play well with the MAGAs. But you could see why an orange narcissist might feel confident to throw around accusations of madness, resting safe in the knowledge that he has passed the highest level of cognitive test known to man – 'person, woman, man, camera, TV'. Basically, a very stable genius.

In *Jane Eyre*, Bertha is also written as being angry. Jealous of Jane, furious at Rochester, lashing out violently at her brother, Mr Mason. Anger is an emotion women are not meant to feel, and these days, the most damning thing a woman in power can see in the press is a snapshot of her looking angry – shouting or scowling. Where angry men are more often perceived as strong and passionate, angry women are seen as out of control, hysterical, overwrought. But the truth is we have every reason to be angry, not least Bertha whose husband locked her in an attic for her whole life and tried to marry the nanny.

When, in 2018, investigative journalist Carole Cadwalladr uncovered an eye-opening scandal involving the work of Cambridge Analytica in swaying the Brexit vote, then-BBC journalist Andrew Neil knew that calling her a 'mad cat woman' on Twitter would diminish her accusations more effectively than just denying them. He was repeating the slurs of Brexiteer, UKIP-funding millionaire and friend-of-Trump Arron Banks, who has repeatedly called her 'crazy cat lady' as have hundreds of likeminded Twitter trolls. The well-trodden 'crazy cat lady' trope is yet another layer in the madwoman puzzle and brings up the inherent mistrust society has for women who remain single. Possibly also a fear of cats, but I think that's very understandable – cats will one day rise up and rule over us, and I don't trust them an inch. But back to the single woman: What is she up to on her own? Skulking around without a partner? Loitering? What does she want? She is either a husband-stealer or insane. The same suspicion is rarely aimed at single men. In the words of Elvis Presley's 'Woman Without Love', 'a man without love is only half a man, but a woman is *nothing at all*'.[23]

In the 19th century, there was a re-emergence of insanity being seen as a peculiarly female thing – a 'female malady', you know, like bad driving, thrush or turning an ankle in the rain. The irrational behaviour known as 'hysteria' – named after the Greek for 'of the womb' – has been considered a female problem ever since the Egyptians first wafted perfume near a depressed woman's vagina to reposition her uterus. (True.) It was Freud and his colleagues who really hammered home the link between madwomen and sex. Notably, madness in a woman has nearly always been 'diagnosed' by a man, and those men have notably connected it with the side of women they have never been able to fathom – female sexuality. It's this revolutionary theory that enabled Freud to start spanking Keira Knightley and get away with it. Psychiatry in the 17th century came to analyse the causes of madness in men and women. In men, the practice cited a vast range of causes: grief, guilt, impotence, abuse, phobia, jealousy and trauma, while the *singular* cause of madness in women was prescribed as Sexual Excess, which I'm pretty sure was a pop group in the '80s.

Western society and science had always veered away from delving too far into the sexual needs of women, and before Freud, hardly acknowledged the existence of it. Freud acknowledged women's sexual needs (cheers, Freud) but also believed women were totally ruled by them. In his paper 'The Psychical Consequences of the Anatomical Distinction between the Sexes', he wrote: 'Women oppose change, receive passively, and add nothing of their own' (fuck you, Freud).

While, mostly, denying the existence of sexual needs in white women, Western culture has fetishised Black women for hundreds of years, during European colonialism – talk of 'virgin land' was not an

201

empty metaphor – it was as if the women found on these new lands were part of the deal, there to be claimed and conquered like the land they lived on. In *Jane Eyre*, Rochester's wife is described as racially 'impure' as she is of Creole heritage and also perceived as overly sexual. She is 'a wife intemperate and unchaste'. This sexual side of her is inextricably linked to her insanity, and also to her race; it is hinted that 'exotic' climates breed women of unpredictable temperaments and unacceptable levels of sexuality. Female sex drives, insanity and non-Western cultures are all inextricably linked together, resulting in characters that can be perceived as *other* – so *other* that Victorian readers, and many today, could read about Bertha without having a moral crisis about her situation.

Women have always had to tread the careful line between being inherently sexual – and available for sex – but not showing that or wanting more than any given man can offer them. The need for sexual satisfaction has, for men, been called a natural instinct (even as a defence for infidelity), while the drive for sexual satisfaction, or even just a joyful celebration of it, for women has frequently been treated as a madness.

Catherine the Great was a queen who quite openly had several lovers throughout her reign, knew how to use sex to her advantage and was a powerful, successful monarch. Her power scared men, and her sexuality made her an easy target for slurs and vitriol. Her neighbour Frederick the Great (there was a real shortage of royal nicknames in those days) wrote: 'A woman is always a woman and, in feminine government, the cunt has more influence than a firm policy guided by straight reason.' See how he pitted women, feminine governing and 'cunt' against 'reason'. And not in a fun R&B lyrics way – 'hey grrrl, that pussy makin me craaazy' – but more of a 'sexually engaged women are the opposite of sane, clear thinking' way, which is much less catchy as a lyric. This led to all sorts of vicious, ludicrous rumours about her that last to this day – most prominently that she died from being shagged by a horse. In the words of Latrice Royale, 'the shade of it all!' There's no evidence that Horsegate is true. A strong, healthy woman enjoying her position and, I guess, various positions, throughout her life? 'Yeah, but she fucked a horse, so.'

Sometimes, women *are* crazy – if we take 'crazy' as having mental health problems. It's worth looking at what, and who, drove some women to these problems, and often when we write off a woman as crazy, what we are observing is a woman in great distress and in need of help. Bertha, by the time we meet her, does seem convincingly 'mad' – she's raging, violent and almost mute apart from screaming. And her hair – don't forget her hair – 'dark, grizzled hair, wild as a mane'. Ladies, DO control your hair; it is the first giveaway of madness. But it's worth asking what happened to Bertha along the way. Sold off to another country by her family, treated with suspicion due to her heritage and her mother's alleged madness, locked up, hidden, drugged.

Take Marilyn Monroe, Judy Garland or Amy Winehouse. All were painted in the press as being unstable in the years leading up to their deaths; their erratic behaviour fuelled headlines and inspired biopics and filled magazine shelves. But if they *were* unstable, it's worth looking at *why*. Garland was deliberately hooked onto barbiturates by the studio system from the age of 12. She was addicted by 15, overworked and constantly sexually assaulted throughout her teenage years, and said she was physically abused by two of her husbands. Monroe was sexually abused by her foster father, married at 16 and when she joined the studio system, again, carefully introduced to a cocktail of uppers and downers provided by her bosses, who also passed her around sexually. Winehouse also found fame young and was addicted to drugs. At points where she should have been getting help, it was reported that her father encouraged her to continue working and touring, and her husband Blake provided her with heroin even when she was in rehab. These were women who were in need of great help but who were instead manipulated, used and mocked for being crazy. So, the label of craziness is used to distract from the needs of distressed women and the causes of their distress (often mistreatment by men), or it's a tool used to take power away from them. Sometimes a mixture of the two. While we're still pissed in the attic, let's look at some other alleged lady nutcases.

Rose McGowan and Alyssa Milano were both accused of being crazy during the course of the #MeToo campaign that activist Tarana Burke first initiated in 2006, and their campaigning to bring Harvey Weinstein to justice. Milano was even accused of being insane when she spoke about her experience of long Covid and Rose McGowan for shaving her head. In fact, women's hairstyles have long been an indicator of insanity, from it being too loose (Ophelia), too long (crazy cat ladies), too short (slutty flappers) or too gone (Sinead O'Connor).

When Christine Blasey Ford accused US Supreme Court nominee Brett Kavanaugh of sexual assault, she was able to remain calm, professional and rational in court. His statement on the other hand was furious and volatile; he even later said his testimony 'might have been too emotional'. A woman could never wield 'over emotional' as a *defence* – for women it is an accusation; it would destroy a woman's testimony. It speaks a lot of Kavanaugh's privilege that he was able to recuse himself of aggressive behaviour by admitting he was too emotional. In any case, and in spite of their respective behaviour in court, it was Blasey Ford who was accused of lying and even insanity. Various conservatives questioned her ability to recall her own assault: former US Attorney Joe DiGenova called her 'a loon' and said one of the signs of lunacy is 'believing something that isn't real'. Brett Kavanaugh's nomination was confirmed and he is now an Associate Justice of the Supreme Court of the United States.

Anita Hill was a law professor who accused US Supreme Court nominee Clarence Thomas of sexual harassment in 1991. She gave clear testimony, and she passed a polygraph test. Thomas was not asked to do a polygraph test. Thomas, who is Black, railed against her accusations calling the case a 'lynching against uppity Blacks', despite the fact that Anita Hill is Black. (The committee hearing her case was made up of 14 white men, naturally.) Her treatment during the case is an absolute smorgasbord of misogynistic accusations – it gets all the ticks – she's mad, she's gay, she's Black, she's slutty, she's evil. During the trial, John Doggett, a Yale classmate of Clarence Thomas's was allowed to give sworn testimony accusing Hill of erotomania – not a fun new rollercoaster at Thorpe Park, but a delusion whereby Hill had fantasised about and fabricated Thomas's romantic interest in her 'when in fact no such interest existed'. Hill was accused of confusing real life with what she'd seen on film. Orrin Hatch, a Republican Senator, questioned the truth of Hill's story because a part of it bore some similarity to a line in *The Exorcist*. (Notably not the head-twisting projectile vomming bit. That probably *would* seem odd in a written testimony of workplace harassment.) The conservative press called Hill 'a lesbian acting out' (which perhaps doesn't sit comfortably with the adjacent accusation of her fantasising over Clarence Thomas) and the same journalist, David Brock, called her 'a little bit nutty and a little bit slutty'.[24] It all adds up to the idea that women causing trouble are crazy, over-sexed and irrational, not to mention that Black women and gay women should know their place. Clarence Thomas's nomination was confirmed and he is now an Associate Justice of the Supreme Court of the United States.

Martha Mitchell was the wife of John Mitchell, the US Attorney under Nixon. Mitchell had a reputation for being outspoken with the press, and when she found out about the Watergate break-in, she called the United Press. At this moment she was kidnapped and then brutally beaten. To cast aspersions on her story, Nixon and his aides told the press she had a drinking problem and that she was convalescing in a psychiatric hospital. She was thought to be an attention-seeking madwoman, and she was disowned by all family except her son. It was three years later that a CIA officer admitted that she was 'basically kidnapped' and corroborated her entire story.

Her experience gave name to a very common but under-acknowledged phenomenon – Martha Mitchell syndrome. This happens when someone describes certain events that, to the listener, seem surprising or hard to believe, and, consequently, that someone is wrongly diagnosed as being insane or delusional when the events are in fact, true. It is, I guess, accidental gaslighting, but an experience common to any woman who has spoken of being raped and been met with doubt and disbelief. The bar for madness is much lower for women than it is for men. For men to be seriously thought of as mad, they have usually killed several people, eaten their own cat or done a series of haggard televised rants drawling about how they have tiger blood in them. Even then, they might be deemed eccentric. A woman might just tell someone that a man once put his hand on her arse and she risks being labelled delusional.

I appreciate this has become less of an appreciation of the book *Jane Eyre* and more of a public health warning, but I believe it can be both. If Radio 4 ever gives me a *Desert Island Discs* slot, *Jane Eyre* will be my chosen book. It's brilliant but complicated as it helped to shape the madwoman trope in a really big way. In how she portrayed Bertha, Charlotte Brontë almost certainly *was* guilty of adding to a societal prejudice against women, and it's worth asking how this particular madwoman in the attic – Bertha – shaped the minds of men and women in the years to come. But let's not forget that Brontë herself was influenced by centuries of sexist, alarmist beliefs about women's psychology, from the ancient Egyptians to Greek tragedies. It's up to you whether you can read *Jane Eyre* with an awareness of all this, of who Bertha might have been and how she was looked at. Brontë's use of the 'madwoman' raises that big question: If art is 'of its time', is it still worthwhile? Can a book still be good if it represents outmoded representations of women or minorities? It isn't really a yes or no answer. But I'd find it hard not to recommend *Jane Eyre*. It contains so much that IS useful, important and inspiring, that, unlike, its madwoman character, it doesn't deserve to be consigned to the attic.

When you see a woman being labelled 'mad', 'crazy', 'insane' or 'psycho', ask yourself some questions. Is this woman a threat? Has she pissed off the person saying it? Is she trying to call out an injustice or uncover something corrupt, and is her accuser involved in that corruption?

Is she crazy or is she angry?

Is she crazy or is she loud?

Is she crazy or is she just refusing to go away?

Is she crazy or is she being too sexy?

Is she crazy or has she just changed her hair a bit too suddenly for you?

And if she does seem a bit crazy – what made her so? What was done to her to get her there?

The madwoman is not just a trope from a gothic horror, not just a monster to fear and forget; she's a weapon and a warning, and she could be any of us.

If you do find a 'madwoman' in your attic, offer her a drink, listen to her and for God's sake let her out. She's probably not mad. She's probably just annoyed at being in your attic, a bit cold and appalled by your lack of insulative heating provision and cackling at your box of retro porn she's found in the eaves.

And maybe heed the advice of this chapter. Just don't go in the loft when you're pissed. Especially if you're a woman, slurring your words slightly and with messy hair. Because then, it might not be what's up there that scares you. You might hear the door getting locked behind you.

207

Only indulge in something you Really like

I think this is great advice. At first glance I thought it was mainly advice about cake, but when you look harder it is a great guideline for everything in life.

It reminds me of a system that my friends and I invented at university called the Calorie-Price-Pleasure Ratio. I put on the standard stone (and a half) in weight during my first year at uni back in 2002, and it took me a surprisingly long time to make the clever calculation that eating a full bowl of porridge with generous dollops of golden syrup, not only for breakfast but as a rudimentary dessert course for *every* meal of the day, might result in some physical change. I had developed this particular eating habit for quite rational reasons: I've always loved very sweet things better than anything savoury. Growing up, I would ask my mum 'What's for afters?' while still finishing off my peas, because I thought then, and I *still* believe, that 'afters' is the best bit of a meal. So, in those first student years of sudden freedom and getting to make my own choices about things like that, I quite understandably decided I could finally do what I wanted: have something sweet after every meal and maybe also in between. However, I had to do so within the confines of what I could afford. With this choice, I had nailed student frugality; porridge oats and a bulk buy of syrup could last weeks, and so were a cheaper alternative than packets of cakes or biscuits. So, began the porridge habit, and it was my daily routine for some months. What resulted from this was a blood sugar level to rival Willy Wonka and me joining the local Weight Watchers at the age of 19.[*]

I wasn't alone – a couple of friends had also put on a 'mystery' 20 pounds – so, we looked around to see if we could make a change, and we did eventually start to suspect the oaty culprit. So, we set about deciding what to replace our porridge habit with. We liked most sweet things but didn't *love* all sweet things. We didn't *love*, for example, porridge and golden syrup. It satisfied that craving for something sweet but it wasn't quite a *treat*. And it was pretty bad for us in those quantities, but, on the other hand it was cheap, which gave it an added gold star – we were all broke. But on the other, other hand, it was only mediocre in terms of pleasure. The golden snitch of treats was something cheap and absolutely delicious, but that wouldn't result in early onset diabetes. And so, we invented the Calorie-Price-Pleasure Ratio.

The idea was that you mentally balanced up the price of food against how healthy it was and against how much joy it brought you. I suppose we anticipated Marie Kondo's 'Does it Spark Joy?' test but with sponge puddings instead of bed linen. The CPP Ratio was really just a bit of fun, rather than a scientific endeavour, and we were arts students, so we didn't adhere strict mathematic values to it, but even loosely applied, it worked. Take a Tunnock's teacake.

Tunnock's Teacakes versus Digestives were a useful comparison: Tunnock's Teacakes are more expensive than Digestives and are about a third more calories per biscuit, but they are WILDLY

---

[*] This was the Cowley Central Weight Watchers group in Oxford run by a lady called Carol who gave us a lecture about bread, while holding a loaf of bread, on my first and only session. My friend Morven and I only attended one session because it became clear that we were instantly hated and rightly so. The local group was attended by grown-up women, mostly over 50, who were facing a lifelong goal of losing weight, and here were two giggly Oxford students with the enviable elasticity of 19-year-olds, who had only recently tilted their BMI into 'overweight' and had done so in a manner which was very obvious to spot and easily reversible. We left before we were thrown out.

nicer to eat than digestives. So, for me, Tunnock's were worth an expense and an indulgence. This all might sound quite purist and abstemious (it must be said that my friend Morven and I, the two principle adherents to the ratio, were brought up Quaker and Methodist, respectively), but it was a good system because it didn't mean you stopped having really nice things to eat, it just meant when you did have something sweet, you ate nicer things that you really enjoyed. It essentially upped our game in the 'afters' stakes, and the fact that it curbed our exponentially rising weight did help a bit.*

What came out of it was positive: a way of not over-spending† or over-indulging unless it was worth something to you. Tunnock's will always be worth it to me. The idea works well for other things in life too, and the calorie idea can be replaced with a health or usefulness score. With that in mind, you might decide smoking cigarettes isn't worth it: it can be *really* pleasurable but it's bad for you AND expensive. Or you might decide the pleasure of smoking outweighs the other things. That's up to you. And the principle works both ways: if you had quite a low pleasure gauge about certain things – have the cheap one. I, for example, have almost no instinct about wine. For me, wine has always fallen into two distinct taste categories:

1. This is nice.
2. This will do.

---

* It is worth adding that while we gained weight, other fellow students lost weight to a dangerous degree. It can be an anxious time, leaving home for the first time, full of pressures to be the 'right' size, when really no such size exists. I don't think we were wrong to want to get more control of our bodies and our eating at that time, but those feelings are rarely isolated and both of us have gone too far in the other direction at different points in our life. The journey to feeling totally happy in your skin is a long one, and I don't know anyone who's really reached that yet.
† I'd be interested to know if the idea has any merit to people who have never had to consider how much money they spend. I think I'll always have a frugal little banker at the back of my head saying 'be careful'.

. . . so, an expensive wine was always wasted on me; I'd rather save my money for other things, like Tunnock's Teacakes. Some people might get a real spark from, say, wearing a very nice expensive pair of shoes that someone else might consider very low on the useful scale – but if you absolutely love them, buy the shoes. Others don't care what's on their feet but really appreciate a fine wine, so distribute your wages accordingly. The best thing about it is, it's only governed by your own measuring stick, not anyone else's.

I mentioned I was brought up in the Methodist church. I don't think I ever properly believed in the literal bits of Christianity – the God of the Old Testament, Jesus being his son, the virgin birth, the miracles or the rising from the dead. But I have always had respect for some of the ideas that came out of the New Testament, and specifically, the ideas that came out of Methodism. It's not all about banning alcohol. Methodism is based on a belief that you should practise moderation in all aspects of life. Not abstinence, moderation. And, taken in the right way, that leads to some very good things.

That principle disapproves of anyone being super-rich. It doesn't support idealistic beauty standards. It encourages taking only as much as you need. It warns against addiction, excessive pride or staying in the sauna too long. To my mind, it even warns against excessive religious zealotry – hold your beliefs, but lightly.

As I've gotten older, moderation in all things doesn't quite fit with my thinking. Moderation is good but not at all times, in all things. I think that there has to be room in life for indulgence, for excess. For falling giddily, head over heels in love, for getting drunk, for eating insanely delicious things with no nutritional content, for bingeing an entire season of *Game of Thrones* over a weekend, for laughing at a private joke until your sides hurt and everyone is staring at you.

There has to be room in life for these things. But if you did them all the time, your life would be mad and they'd lose their specialness. Which brings us back to moderation. I suppose my principle in life is moderation (in moderation).

Indulge. But indulge in moderation. Moderate yourself, but not too much.

All of which is much more neatly summed up in the advice on this small piece of paper.

Only indulge in things you really like.

And I really like this advice.

Don't sleep with the bassist

I disagree. Bass players are likely to be dependable, quietly confident, a team player, not attention-seeking and have good rhythm and skillful hands.

If anything, avoid the lead singer.

Sincerity is key. You have to be able to fake sincerity

A good joke, but also, I think, true.

Perhaps the writer of this advice was paraphrasing the French diplomat and dramatist Jean Giraudoux, who said: 'The key to success is sincerity. If you can fake that you've got it made.' It was later appropriated by the American comic George Burns.

And they're right. Faking sincerity is crucial in all walks of life and for good and wholesome reasons. You could call faking sincerity 'acting' or 'pretending' or 'lying', but you could also call it diplomacy, kindness, tact, negotiation, flirtation or well-developed social skills.

Times I Have Been Insincere

Told a children's choir, shortly before a big performance, that they sounded great when let me tell you they did not.

Told a friend I enjoyed reading their book when let me tell you I did not ... read it.

Expressed interest while my friend told me in detail about the fittings and finishes of her new kitchen island (ivory granite FYI).

Told my husband that his bald patch has NOT gotten bigger since his last haircut.

Exaggerated my enthusiasm for classical opera when applying for an admin job at The Classical Opera Company.

Exaggerated my enthusiasm for Prince in the early stages of dating a die-hard Prince fan (now husband, balding).

Laughed deliberately louder at a new comedian's gig, among a very difficult audience.

Told my mum she looks 20 years younger than she is (she actually looks 15 years younger than she is).

Typed the words 'can't wait!' at the end of thousands of work-related emails.

The list could go on, and is, as I hope you'd agree, harmless, or even for the best.

I think any person has good reasons for occasional insincerity in general life – an encouraging teacher, a bored blue plaque tour guide, a politician showing basic levels of respect to the leader of a country whose nuclear bombs could wipe out half the world.

Classic novels, folk tales, Disney films and reality TV shows have long championed the vital qualities of being always-always-truthful and sincere to a fault. But there's a difference between telling the truth when it matters, and telling your truth, all the time, without being asked. The quality of honesty has been remoulded, rebranded in the last few decades into the fresh hell of being, not simply honest, but #NoFilter. Having #NoFilter is a terrible idea. Filters are important. Filters are what make you a bearable person and, on a grander scale, stop wars happening. Filters are a crucial part of human communication. Being brutally honest, rude or no-holds-barred confrontational is now often mistakenly seen as a good thing, especially for entertainment value.

We've watched with half-glee half-horror, the reality stars who are 'just me, sorry, that's just me, that's who I am, I say it like it is and if you don't like it then sorry but that's just me and I say what I think if you can't handle it get out of the kitchen or something?'

One of my guilty pleasures is a reality show called *Selling Sunset* on Netflix; a programme in which a cabal of shiny, eight-foot tall, surgically enhanced Amazons divide their working week between selling multi-million-dollar homes in the Hollywood Hills, talking shit about whichever of them is currently absent and talking shit directly to their faces. As I'm sure the producers intended, it's almost a morality tale, and the moral is that both of these states – extreme insincerity and extreme sincerity – are unhelpful and do more harm than good.

That balance becomes even more important in politics. We think we admire politicians who never ever lie (but vote in ones who constantly do), but while we do want politicians who are sincere, what we need more is a politician who can get the job done and sometimes getting the job done means employing the appearance of sincerity, when called for. It takes intelligence, good judgement and tact, but it only works if you actually have some basic moral values, so this subtle and occasional use of insincerity doesn't really work for the current UK cabinet, who have nothing to be sincere or insincere about, operating, as they do, on a total lack of principles except a blind and vacuous loyalty to Boris Johnson, a man who isn't even sincere about his own fucking hair.

No-one's advocating being fake and phoney all day every day. It's not a lifestyle choice, or at least, it shouldn't be. On the whole, telling the truth is good and important. It feels better; it's clearly the best resting state. But the occasional soupçon of fakery can be useful, kind, even necessary.

So, the next time your friend tearfully shows you the 12th photo of their new baby and it's identical to the previous 11, and says 'isn't she beautiful' even though, as in all the photos before, she is still a weird-looking scrunched up purple ball covered in yellow stuff, I hope you remember to be wonderfully, and generously, insincere.

Smile as much as possible

This is not good advice and if you can't work out why I'm not going to tell you.

Okay, fine; I'll tell you.

I have what many now call a 'resting bitch face'. This lovely phrase means that, at rest, in its default position, my face doesn't fall naturally into the open, friendly demeanour of a woman who is ready to embrace a Labrador or serve you a cold beer, but instead looks like I'm gearing up to interview a war criminal.

The phrase 'resting bitch face' has arisen in the last few years, and it's not surprising that it's gendered – men having a serious resting expression is so normal and expected as to not require any comment but women having a serious resting expression is a phenomenon, something that requires explanation and, to a certain extent, apology.

I know I'm not alone in saying I've been told to smile throughout my life – from the school photographer who kept saying 'more, more, no, a BIG smile, show your teeth!' to the half critiques/half cat-calls of strangers in the street.

I remember a good five years of my childhood when people told me I was smiling wrong. My mouth just didn't fall into the big toothy smile that other kids seemed able to do easily, and when I attempted it, I looked like The Joker. So, I grinned. Mouth clamped shut, I tried just grinning in photos but the person taking the photo would often say I didn't look happy *enough*. School reports consistently described me as 'serious' even though my overriding memories are having fun and joking around with friends. Throughout my career as a comedian, and, I think specifically as a female comedian, I have been repeatedly accused of 'not seeming like a comedian', when people meet me in real life, and when I ask why, the reason is given that, even now, I don't smile enough for the job I do.

From the age of about 12, like many girls, I started getting heckled in the street by men. This wasn't every day – but every few weeks perhaps, walking through town in school uniform or nipping to the shops, and while some were cat calls, other comments ranged from 'cheer up' to 'smile love' to 'it might never happen'.

Here are my personal feelings about being told by a stranger in the street to smile and, in my life experience, I have only ever seen men shouting at women to do this. When it happens, my inner monologue goes into overdrive even though my face is a mask of disinterest.

1. 'Smile love!' At what? Smile at WHAT? What are you suggesting I smile at? You? Why would I smile at you? You are a strange man who is shouting out at me in the street; that doesn't make me happy. Smile at what? The weather? We are in the UK; it is middling at best. Smile at what? The likelihood of continuing Tory rule? The number of jobs Amanda Holden gets offered? My ticking body clock? Smile at what? At nothing? Just walk around grinning for no reason? Not even *you* are doing that. Looking around me, no-one is doing that, so why are you suggesting I do it?! (I know why! Because on some level you consider women ornamental and not as an equal human being with their own inner life. Am I close?)

2. 'It might never happen!' For all you know, it has happened. It almost certainly has. What an incredibly bold assumption to make – that the stranger you're calling out to, has had NO bad experiences, in their past OR recently. Nothing to be concerned about – the only difficult things in my life are yet to come, if ever. 'It might never happen' – 'It' being, presumably, anything that might cause me to have an expression other than smiling. That 'it', therefore, could range from trying to remember what to buy in the shop to realising I've forgotten my niece's birthday, from being worried about a friend or having bad period pain to the death of a loved one. I fantasise about marching up to you and

223

giving you a long list of things that have 'happened' to me to make you feel terrible about your behaviour. But the truth is, my dream scenario, where you go red, look sad and are profoundly moved by what I've said and vow never to do it again, would never happen. You'd just ask if I was 'on the blob or something' and walk off.

3. 'Cheer up love.' Ironically I was quite cheerful until I walked down this street and I clocked you/and your friend(s) standing against the wall, looking out at people, and I felt intimidated. I anticipated the possibility of being called at or approached. So, I walked a bit faster, drew my coat around me a bit tighter, wore a neutral expression and glanced down at my phone to make it look like I was busy. At other times, I might put earphones in to show I won't hear anything you say or start rooting around in my bag to avoid being engaged by anything. I am prepped for avoidance and already I am actively trying to neither interest you nor anger you. All this has happened in a couple of seconds, and I am concentrating, hoping nothing happens. You shout out 'cheer up love'. But I haven't reached you yet, I still have to walk past you. I'm currently on your side of the street. Do I cross the street to be further away from you or will that draw attention and make it seem like I'm scared? I am a bit scared. I stay on the path and walk past, and you say 'smile' again as I pass you. You want me to address it – with a smile or talk or just anything, but I don't, I keep looking forward and ignoring you which pisses you off, and, once I'm a few metres away I hear you mutter something including 'bitch'.

Those are just a few examples of what can happen, often and eas- ily, that we don't bother recounting because it's normal life. Telling women to smile for you is an aggression. Shouting at strangers about their face isn't okay. You don't know what they're experiencing or thinking but you believe they have a duty to smile for you, because you view them as an ornament. Well, we don't always want to smile, and we especially don't want to smile at you. Fuck off.

Western society has quite the pre-occupation with putting on a smile. From war to heartbreak, there is a cultural touchstone suggesting we smile through it all. British wartime songs like 'Pack Up Your Troubles' suggested soldiers should smile, smile, smile, as they make the journey to the front line while 'Wish Me Luck As You Wave Me Goodbye' asked loved ones to not cry, but to cheer and smile as they left. This went alongside wartime propaganda campaigns like Britain's now repopularised 'Keep Calm and Carry On' and the US postal service's 'Keep 'Em Smiling'.

After the war, 1950s much-loved American crooner songs like 'When You're Smiling' suggested that you smiling can make the whole world smile, but that, conversely if you cry, you are responsible for bringing on the rain. Similarly, the lyrics to the beautiful ballad 'Smile' sung by Nat King Cole would send shivers down any mental health practitioner's spine. It is a repeated imperative to smile, even though your heart is *breaking*. And don't forget that your children better not cry either, or even pout, if they want to get anything for Christmas, according to 'Santa Claus Is Coming To Town'. These songs are absolute bangers but the message within them is pretty messed up by today's standards of emotional transparency. Britain is so very proud of its stiff upper lip; it's surprising our National Anthem is so entirely about the queen and the colonies and not just something like:

'When all your hope has gone,
Do not show anyone!
Smile through the paaaain, dadadada . . .'

225

The encouragement to smile and be cheerful in spite of dire circumstances is unhelpful for different social groups in distinct ways. In line with the damaging gender stereotypes we are all familiar with, women have long been expected to provide smiles and cheer while men have been expected to be stoical and strong. This starts as children: girls are disproportionately told off for being moody or bossy, angry or aggressive while boys are indulged in those behaviours; meanwhile, the idea of 'boys don't cry' persists as a trend in raising children.

I spoke to Amy Cooke-Hodgson, who is a primary school teacher, improv teacher and educational facilitator, about her experiences with children in schools. She said, 'I think schools are getting better at giving children space to process their emotions in a safe way' but she added that it hasn't always been like this and often still isn't. 'I have in the not-so-distant past experienced adults saying things like 'be a big boy, don't cry' and 'don't be a crybaby' when boys are processing a sad or stressful experience.' On the other end of that treatment, while girls might be treated more sympathetically when they cry, Cooke-Hodgson suggests in many cases, anger in boys is tolerated more easily than anger in girls – 'You'll often hear comments like "he gets very worked up at playtime because he's so competitive"' – but she suggests that justification isn't applied to girls – 'I'm not sure I've heard an angry girl being described as competitive.'

So, emotional displays like anger or joy are treated differently as children get older, and that is carried into adulthood. While girls and women have been more encouraged to smile a lot, boys and men have been discouraged from crying or showing sadness or emotional struggle. Genuine smiles are always a good thing. Masking your feelings with a smile is rarely a good thing but a hard habit to get out of when we are all so conditioned to do it.

Male suicide rates in the UK are at an all-time high and still growing. There are many complicated factors at play but one on

226

which nearly all mental health charities agree is that men are not used to being open with emotional struggles. There is more onus on men to hold it together, to 'man up'.

Alex Holmes is an author and podcaster who campaigns for male mental health, and he draws a link between the fact that suicide is now the leading cause of death in men under the age of 45 in the UK and the societal pressures on men to bottle up emotion and seem strong and in control. In his book *Time To Talk*[*] he unpicks six myths that men live with including 'real men don't cry', 'real men don't doubt themselves', 'real men never fail' and how these myths can cause men to feel alienated, lonely and disconnected.

Many of us have been trained from a young age to mask our true emotions by smiling or being cheerful when in fact what we need sometimes is a good cry, a wallow on the sofa or simply to talk about what we are feeling. Smiling is the best way of expressing your happiness, but it's not a great way to hide your troubles, and it has been used over the years to make women feel ornamental and men feel they can't admit they're sad.

Smiles are wonderful. But, and I am starting to hear a running theme through this book, they're not simple. Some are! Some are gloriously simple. A bride smiling as she walks down the aisle. The smile you do when you get your own quid back from returning a trolley. A baby smiling at a fart. But smiles can be complicated, fraught with hidden depth and meaning. Smiling ruefully, smiling sadly, smiling in sympathy, smiling slyly, smiling in victory, smiling at someone else's misfortune. Brief, awkward smiles, long, sleepy smiles. The whole gamut from the full Julia Roberts to the Mona Lisa. And then there's smiling when you don't want to.

I'm a comedian and I'm aware of the irony of saying this when my job seems to be to make people laugh, to put a smile on people's

---

[*] *Time To Talk* by Alex Holmes (Welbeck Balance 2021).

faces. But actually, I feel at my best as a performer when I can make them feel different things too. In the best shows I do, I hope audiences mostly laugh and smile but also experience . . . surprise, defiance, sadness, catharsis, outrage, empathy. There's so much to feel in this world, and we have a million different expressions to show how we feel and showing how we feel is good.

So, smile. Smile if you feel happy, smile when you want to, give toothy smiles, loving smiles, flirty smiles, laughing smiles, I-Can't-Believe-You-Just-Said-That smiles, Go-On-Then-One-More-Slice smiles, I-Love-This-Song smiles and even Oh-Well-That's-Life-I-Guess smiles. But smile on your terms. Smile how you smile. And don't smile whenever you can. Smile whenever you want.

Don't steal from kids

Bit worthy. They're the best targets. There's a reason 'it's like taking candy from a baby' exists as a phrase; it's advice about best practice for theft. And there's no need to feel too guilty – whatever you're taking, let's be honest this child probably didn't buy it themselves. It's the parents who will have to replace it, so at the end of the day, you're still stealing from adults, so this is, frankly, a non-issue as far as I'm concerned.

Follow your first instinct

Terrible, terrible advice. That's what zombies and dogs and those guys who stormed the capitol do. We can do better. Think it through. Note your first instinct; pay it some attention. And then have a ponder and actively form a decision. Do better than your pet or that guy in the horns and the furry hat. Filter out things based on mania or sexual aggression or greed or fury – don't go around smashing things unless you definitely mean to. Your first instinct when someone bashes into you in the street might be to confront them angrily but thinking twice or looking again, they might be a vulnerable person, a tired or ill or disabled person or they might be much bigger and scarier than you in which case, probably best to keep walking. Your first instinct one hour into an incredibly boring play might be to shout MAKE IT STOP and leg it mid-scene but that would ruin a lot of people's night. Wait for the scene-break at least. The first instinct of a drunk teenager playing around on a rooftop might be 'I can definitely make that jump' – they probably can't and shouldn't try. You might, during your life, have instincts to lash out at strangers or shout at kids, your own or someone else's, or to suddenly try to kiss the new girl at work or to advise someone on weight loss or to lift a crazy big weight in the gym without anyone spotting you or to eat an entire swiss roll in one sitting followed by a pint of chocolate milk or arrest the suspect you've had a hunch about all through this goddamned case, even though they have an alibi and there's no evidence. Some (some) of these things might be the right thing to do once you've had a good think about it (swiss rolls are arguably a single serving), but some definitely aren't. So, do the work. Make an active decision. Weigh things up. Don't be brain lazy. Enjoy being human.

Be Kind

Be Kind.
Be Kind.
Be Kind.

When you repeat any word too many times, it starts to lose all meaning.

'velvet'
'velvet'
'velvet'
'wait, VELLvet?'
'VELVETT'
'velvt'

And for me the same has happened with 'Be Kind'. I've lost the sense of it.

'B'kinned'? 'Beck'ned'? 'Beak-innd'? Because 'Be Kind' has, in recent years, gone from being a fairly universal and obvious goal for how to treat others, into an over-hyped, over-marketed mantra. It is a movement, a hashtag, an online identifier, used in so many wildly opposing contexts that I don't quite know what to make of it anymore.

I got a lot of kindness-based pieces of advice from audience members in my shows, ranging from 'Follow your heart but be mindful, tolerant and kind' to 'Always be nice – you never know what someone has to go home to . . .' to the inarguable 'Don't be A Dick' (written in beautiful calligraphy), as well as the simplest and most enduringly popular 'Be Kind'. So, I wanted to take a few pages to explore the advice and the branded powerhouse that is Be Kind, #BeKind and BeKind.

Kindness: /ˈkʌɪn(d)nəs/
Noun
the quality of being friendly, generous, and considerate.

Being kind seems, undoubtedly, like the right way to behave. Of course, we should be kind. We're told to be kind from the very start – it's in Ladybird books, it's in school hymns, it's in all the holy books, it's in Shakespeare, it's what parents repeat to their toddlers in the sand-pit. It's on fridge magnets and in the sentimental moral lessons at the end of American sitcoms. It's The Good Samaritan. It's 'The quality of mercy is not strained', it's The BFG, it's Chandler paying Joey's rent for the best part of a decade.

It costs nothing to be kind
Cruel to be kind
The Kindness of Strangers
To kill with kindness
Kindness costs nothing
#BeKind

I'm pro-kindness. Obviously. I think nearly everyone is. But kindness, for nearly everyone, is something we all believe we are already doing. Apart from some very troubled outliers, kindness is a given – we all think we are practising it as a default setting. I don't know any one of us who gets home and crows over the pleasure of not giving anything to a homeless person or fondly reminisces about treading on an intern's foot or revels in having made a child cry. I mean, we've all had a PE teacher who seemed to enjoy making us bawl our eyes out but I now think *even* some of them had good intentions at heart.

Most people are aiming for kindness. The difficulty lies in how we interpret 'kind'. It isn't an absolute. So, working under the hallowed philosophical position of #BeKind doesn't actually guide you in any particular direction; it can mean totally different things to different people. That's why I'm so averse to it being posted with no context and no specificity.

You *shouldn't* always be kind. Whether you live by the teaching of Christ or the Qur'an or the lyrics to 'Turn! Turn! Turn!' by the Byrds, it's not natural or helpful to be peaceful and kind all the time; there's a season for all things. Sometimes Fairness is more important than Kindness. There's a clear place for fairness within the judicial system and rehabilitation and consequences for wrongdoing. But, whether you're faced with a genocidal regime, an abusive partner or simply someone who is legislating against your rights, what is needed, more than Kindness, is Opposition. Anger, then resolve, then firmness, then action. Kindness has a place but if we're talking about it in practice, in real life, rather than hypothetically and in a utopia, then sometimes we need other behaviours first.

#BeKind is not useful advice, because it's not always obvious which action is the kindest. You can be a kind person, but that doesn't mean you're kind all the time; in fact, you can't be.

Kindnesses rub up against each other, just as rights rub up against each other.

Is it kinder to remove a violent bully from a school, who has hurt several classmates, or to let him stay, while he's a danger to the others? Perhaps excluding him means he's at home with abusive parents or perhaps excluding him puts strain on his already desperate parents – what would be kindest for them? What is kind to those who have been hurt by him? And might be, in the future?

Is it kinder to campaign for a socialist government who will protect the poorest or kinder to spend 10 hours of your week doing voluntary charity work?

235

Is it kinder to give your children lots of toys and money so they are happy or to give them less, so they are more grounded and learn what it means to earn something?

When you feel down, is it kinder to keep yourself in a state of cosy indulgence, eating whatever you fancy and curled up on the sofa? Or is it kinder to make yourself eat healthily and get out for walks even if you don't feel like it?

Is it kind to give sweets to children?

If you adopt a dog but live in a small flat, is it kind to take on an unwanted dog or is it unkind because there's not much room for it?

Is it kindness to contact your friend a lot when they're going through tragedy or to give them space?

Is it kinder to let Jean Valjean steal a loaf of bread for his starving family or is it kinder to return that bread to its rightful owner?

Is it kinder to lead your student friends into a revolutionary battle for their rights, knowing they might die or to let them disperse peacefully, knowing they'll live, but under an unfair regime?

Is it kinder to tell your adopted daughter the truth about her mother's tragic death or to let her live without the burden of it?

It's possible I've got a bit stuck on *Les Misérables* here – it's happened before; you'll have to excuse me.

I don't think there is a definitive answer to any of these; there is an intent to do good on both sides. Morality, ethics and the right thing to do; these are all complicated. That's why bearded old men tried to figure out the 'right answer' for thousands of years and none of them could categorically find one.*

#BeKind isn't just meaningless, I think it can be harmful. You will see those words written in the bios and on the Instagram stories of people from all walks of life – from body positive campaigners to Trump fanatics, from animal rights activists to libertarians, from

---

* Perhaps if they'd asked more women they might have got closer.

pro-life campaigners to pro-choice campaigners. In my time doing satire on *The Mash Report*, I criticised Piers Morgan for being too kind to Trump in an interview, because Trump's actions are so deeply unkind, and when I did so, I was accused by many of being unkind to Morgan and unkind to Trump and was told this in ways which were very unkind to me.

I received an email where the body of the message read simply 'Try to be nicer' and the subject line was 'From your Twitter feed you appear to be a bit of a cunt'.

And it often comes up in politics. In response to the murder of MP Sir David Amess in 2021, people like MP Mark Francois and Commons Speaker Sir Lindsay Hoyle called for a kinder political discourse, despite the fact that Francois himself had fired up rage over Brexit with language like saying 'We are signing your death warrant' to a Brexit protestor and comparing EU officials to Hitler. Calls for kinder politics can come from all sides, but it will never be entirely without agenda and is often hypocritical. Jeremy Corbyn called for a kinder politics.[25] Boris Johnson called for a kinder politics.[26] I don't believe they shared the same end-goal. So, I think it's clear the concept can be stretched and manipulated.

Boris Johnson's request for a 'kinder', more 'civil' debate in politics is a good example of where #BeKind is harmful. It suggests putting a veneer of goodness over something that, in itself, can be extremely unkind in its intent. Political discussions can involve real threat to people's lives; the debates over equal marriage, free school meals for kids, when to go into lockdown and Brexit that won him the election will affect the livelihoods of hundreds of thousands of people, as well as their careers and businesses. To ask people to remain calm and polite in such situations is, in itself, a violence. It is gaslighting. How can you ask a mother whose child now won't have enough food to please be 'kind' in her responses to the minister who voted for that, who has a net fortune of £100 million, went to Eton and lives in a literal castle?* To request kindness from anyone whose life is being debated towards the privileged few debating it, is not in itself a kind thing to do. In fact, it's manipulative and dangerous.

Some of the people who post #BeKind have very good intentions and, like all of us, simply want a better world. Following the tragic death of British TV presenter Caroline Flack in 2020, another, specific, #BeKind movement was launched. Shortly before she died, Flack had posted the following quote on Instagram: 'If you can be anything in this world . . . be kind.' This was picked up by her supporters and #BeKind was spread around in the following weeks, with the specific aim of discouraging the press, and people on social media, from fuelling endless gossip campaigns and harassing celebrities for the sake of clickbait. The discussion surrounding her death compared her situation with that of Amy Winehouse, Marilyn Monroe, Princess Diana – famous women who were followed, hounded and bullied by the press and its readership. The campaign began as a rallying cry around a particular situation; a vulnerable woman driven to desperation by the cruelty of the media. #BeKind in those first few days had that very clear purpose. But it quickly diluted into a more general theme; T-shirts were printed with the slogan and cupcakes were made with the message in icing. Once it becomes too broad and overused, #BeKind becomes impossible to sustain as a goal.

Psychologist Professor Robin Banerjee, who has published articles about social anxiety and the link between kindness and well-being, was quoted in the *Guardian* as saying 'Any campaign to promote kindness has a lot of potential merit, in principle . . . but creating a kind culture, whether at a school, in a workplace or in society more generally, is not easy'.[27] Telling the press to #BeKind in their treatment of famous people who are openly struggling and vulnerable – that is a clear message. But as the campaign gets bigger,

---

* Yes, I'm talking about Jacob Rees-Mogg again but it could as easily be any number of Tory ministers.

we start to lose sight of what specifically prompted it, and so, it starts to lose power and just become a soundbite. As Banerjee puts it: 'Any campaign has got to be more than simply 'telling' people to be kind. It's about changing the contexts in which we live and work.'

So, while #BeKind has the potential for good, it is also susceptible to being misused. Put simply, not everyone who posts #BeKind is kind. Some people hijack campaigns like that for their own publicity or to boost their followership or use the phrase to shame or persuade or manipulate. Ellen Degeneres had a charity scheme called Be Kind and it became a slogan used on much of her merchandise – this is before her show was accused by multiple employees of allowing bullying and creating a toxic workplace. In 2021, influencer Sheridan Mordew was interviewed about how she could justify continuing to go on holidays abroad at the height of the pandemic. She was asked 'so, you believe this travel was essential?' and she replied with 'Well, in a world where you can be anything, be kind'.[28] That's the quote used by Caroline Flack but here it appears to help her avoid answering a difficult question about Covid safety. #BeKind can be used to silence people. It's almost as effective as 'Calm down' in bringing a heated debate to a gut-wrenchingly annoying close. It's hard to come back when someone's told you you're not being kind. Throwing out #BeKind gives you an instant moral superiority without you earning it. And it's effective.

Kindness is vital. Of course, it is. It is a good thing to practise; it is probably the best default setting. I try to be as kind as possible. But I also acknowledge it is not *always* possible or appropriate. The concept of a kindness movement is very appealing – spreading kindness can result in so much good, so much warmth, and I am all for that. But I don't think the #BeKind trend of recent years is achieving that while it is so widely misused and used without any real intent. Simply telling a stranger to #BeKind without context is as meaningless as telling them to #BeAngry or #BeSad or #BeOverjoyed. At whom?

About what? And why? #BeKind is like asking a woman to smile. If a stranger asks that of me, I want to know 'at what'?

The most positive online movements are specific. There are very few successful charities dedicated to 'generally being nice'. To enact change, you need a purpose, a subject, a target. The awareness spread through the Black Lives Matter movement, especially in 2020, was inspiring, active, specific. Those black squares some of us posted on instagram were rightly criticised as 'performative activism' – being seen to do the right thing without putting any thought or effort in. What is more helpful than a black square is a post sharing information, raising money or promoting a Black voice. You had to get your head around what was happening before posting – you had to read and research and then decide what to say and how to act. It wasn't easy to engage with; it required effort and thought.

The stories and righteous anger that were generated by the #MeToo movement, and the real changes resulting from that and the subsequent #TimesUp campaign, were effective. It too was specific and angry and had a clear goal. I remember my feelings around the first days of #MeToo – that really, you couldn't engage with it fully without being honest about your experience. Even if you didn't share your story with the public, it made you think about it privately. Through these campaigns, women recounted and revisited their traumas and many men had to re-examine what the world was really like after seeing friends and family post their stories. It wasn't easy to engage with; it required effort and thought.

Following an attack in Leytonstone in 2015 by a man who claimed to have extremist Islamist influences, the hashtag #YouAintNoMuslimBruv trended in the UK – a uniquely British way of saying: this man doesn't represent our religion. This addressed a painful issue for Muslims across the world, who are drawn into the same bracket as extremists and terrorists by the actions of people who have hijacked their religion. It helped people understand – this is not what Islam is about.

#ReclaimTheseStreets, in the wake of Sarah Everard's murder in 2021, was used to help organise a series of protests and vigils, sign petitions and provide a place to vent about the normalisation of women walking the streets in fear. And following that, the #EveronesInvited Instagram campaign set up by Soma Sara started suddenly receiving thousands of testimonies from schools all over the UK, from girls and boys telling their stories of sexual assault and harassment. It was a true wake-up call to how early it starts, that it is happening in education and how serious the problem is.

These campaigns had a goal and were hugely positive in a very real, practical sense. I think the best way of spreading positivity is this: positivity with purpose.

I'm not saying everything you do online should be hard. I just tweeted about *Married at First Sight Australia* and Instagrammed about having Weetabix for breakfast, and I have no regrets.

Telling people to 'Be Kind', whether it's part of a TV interview, a fixture in your Twitter bio, part of an online campaign or hand-written on a piece of paper, is easy. It's easy to say but it's not easy to follow, without being told more, without the writer putting a bit of effort in. The minute you say it, you're taking a moral stance: so, earn it. Know what behaviour it is that you're judging when you say it, and why you're judging it. Show your workings.

My hope for #BeKind is that it starts being used *within a context*. I won't always like the context. But I will understand it. So, when people tell me to be kinder to Boris Johnson, they'll explain the context and I'll know how to respond. And when people tell journalists to be kinder to Meghan Markle, they'll know what they're talking about. Or when people tell Remainers to be kinder to Brexiteers or tell Brexiteers to be kinder about Remainers or when people say #BeKind at the end of a tweet about veganism or Kanye West or Universal Credit or Children In Need it will have a meaning.

241

I hope it's clear that this chapter isn't anti-kindness. When you boil it down, it's really about online behaviour. Because 'Be Kind' is something that is said a million times more online than it ever would be in 'real life' – to someone's face. If you say to someone out loud in conversation 'Hey, Be Kind'. then you really mean it; that's a strong feeling. If you heard someone say 'Be Kind' to your face after you've done or said something, you would think twice. You would examine your actions. You might get angry or you might feel guilty, but you'd certainly feel it hit home.

Online it is easy to throw out #BeKind to the world and for it to never land anywhere, because it applies to everything and therefore nothing. #BeKinds abound on social media. They are like those floating lanterns you can send off into the night sky: rising up, seen by many and then floating out of sight – with no consequence except the odd small fire.

But a face-to-face, out loud 'Be Kind' is something you very rarely say. I think that's because when you really talk to someone, someone you know, someone whose eyes you can meet, whose body you can read, who is a real, breathing person in front of you, it is far easier to see and understand where that person is coming from and it is far easier to see and understand that by and large, we are all trying our best to be kind already.

Don't let anyone stop you being shiny

Bang on. I think the use of 'shiny' here makes it more specific advice than just 'play nice, kids'. I think whoever wrote it chose the word for a reason. 'Shiny' to me sounds like when you have a real glow, a fizzy joy, a frankly uncool enthusiasm, and how easy it is to let someone dampen that and make you duller and greyer and flatter. I once saw the historian Simon Schama at the centre of a dance floor boogying wildly to Carly Rae Jepson's 'Call Me Maybe'. I didn't expect that. I respected him as a historian and I now respect him as a dancer. He's not talented exactly but he bopped to that tune like the actual Lord of the Dance and he was absolutely electric because he didn't give a flying fuck about anyone watching. Be more Simon Schama.

Stay giddy, stay bright, stay shiny.

Life is but a piss into the winds of time

But what a piss.

Even a small piece of card can make someone feel included

This was one of the most memorable bits of advice I received. I thought about it a lot after the show. Live performance should be about making people feel included. Whether it's comedy, improv, drama, dance, opera or avant-garde physical theatre, it should be about bringing an audience *into* the world – not shutting them out. And if it's avant-garde physical theatre, then lock the doors because people will try to leave. It should make them feel like they are *in on* something that they weren't before, and that they're sharing an experience together – even if that shared feeling is 'what the hell is going on here in this avant garde piece of physical theatre?' or 'I wish we'd stayed in and watched *Drag Race*'.

I jest, of course – avant garde physical theatre can be fun and accessible, just as some stand-up comedy has the potential to alienate. I've watched really fun, exciting, operas – like one that took place in a bar in Soho, while the singers whirl around you and your Bacardi and coke – and I've also literally fallen asleep during a very popular stand-up's most famous routine. I've seen people pissing themselves at a silent Le-Coq style clown show but left cold by a supposedly knockabout improv show in a sports bar. It all depends, and you can't please everyone all the time. If you're pleasing everyone all of the time, you've made the live performance version of 'Baby Shark', and actually now I say that, I realise lots of people really hate 'Baby Shark', so, there's really no hope of universal approval.

But inclusion is a good goal and there are different ways of feeling included in live performance. You might feel included because you're surrounded by people all watching the same thing at the same time; you're sharing a space, sharing what you can see and hear. Even though you're reacting to it differently; you're all choosing to be there, together.

You might feel included by how it makes you feel – you might feel 'seen' for the first time in ages, by what's being shown onstage – it might reflect something you think but haven't been able to express.

Or you might actually be included in the performance.

When you're the one creating standup or improv or theatre there are lots of different ways to interact with the audience, and make them feel included, if you want to. You might chat to the people on the front rows.* This might range from 'what do you do for a living?' to 'who's your favourite member of the Wu-Tang Clan?' or anything in between. You can ask big open questions to the whole crowd and ask them to do a collective cheer just to get them leaning in a bit:

'You feeling good, Latitude? You enjoying the soy lattes?'
'Gimme a cheer if you're drinking!'
'Who's in from Coventry tonight? And who's in from somewhere better?'

You can lead sing-alongs! Audiences think they don't want to do this, but they get really into it. The funniest sing-alongs I've done in my comedy have involved getting different sections of the audience to sing different parts in counterpoint – ha! accidental choir! I got you! Best way to get your endorphins IMO.

---

* Those sitting on the front row at a stand-up show are often either overly fearful of, or overly eager about, being spoken to by the comic. The sweet spot for front row interaction is finding someone who wasn't expecting to be talked to but isn't crippled with embarrassment and who isn't so pissed they try to climb on the stage, start a fight or loudly break up with their girlfriend just as you deliver your punchline (yes, it's happened).

In a lot of improv shows, audience members are asked to shout out suggestions for particular things to put in the scenes and spark the imagination of the players:

'Can I get a film genre?'
'Can you give me a household object?'
'A profession?'

Inevitably a lot of the time someone will take it upon themselves to resolutely reply:

'porno!'
'dildo!'
'prostitute!'

and think they are the funniest person in the room and the first person to have ever thought of these replies. I doubt that person is reading this book, but if you are – we're not intimidated by your replies or embarrassed or stuck; we've just heard them a million times before and are bored by them, that's why we might take some-one else's.* But largely audience shout-outs are brilliant and joyful and makes them part of the show.

There are many ways to encourage audience suggestions and not all audience members feel confident enough to shout out in the middle of a show but might feel more comfortable contribut-ing anonymously. There's also a different type of suggestion that can come if you give someone a minute to think about their answer. That's why, for every show in my 'Keynote' tour, I handed out small

---

* On one occasion at the Comedy Store we did take 'Porno' and we walked through the rudiments of a (fully clothed) porn scene, complete with me, dead-eyed, saying very clearly to the other actor, 'No, I'm not having an orgasm – it's extremely rare for women to come through penetrative sex alone, but thank you for asking.'

bits of card or paper that I'd cut up on the train to audience members. Those little bits of advice are what have formed the backbone of this book. I handed them out as people walked in to take their seats – I gave one card to anyone on their own and anyone in a pair or a group. Sometimes people in a group would ask for extra, and quite often I would say no. Not to be mean but because I hoped they would collaborate together and decide what they wanted to submit. I read every piece of advice I received on a small piece of card or on the back of an envelope or a ticket or a post office notification slip. I was grateful for every one. Even the ones that were heckles.

It is lovely to me that the person who wrote this felt included by being invited to write on a piece of card. And that they did write on it and handed it in. It is no small thing to do, and that's why I valued every one. They feel like treasure.

Many people who came to see the show were reluctant to take one or to write anything down. Lots of people said, 'I can't think of anything' but what that sometimes means is 'I can't think of anything that would be good enough'. But, as in improv, any suggestion is a gift. And any suggestion might be included and be useful and be seen. The clever jokey advice or the profound important advice weren't always the bits that were the most interesting or most useful. When I would read various bits of their advice out, incorporating them into the show, the most enjoyable snippets, for me and the audience, were the unexpected, simple, weird, short, rambling and sometimes even not-advice-at-all.

As a performer, when someone hands back the card and says they don't want to join in, my instinct is to 'help them', to give them confidence in how they might join in, to tell them that there's no contribution that wouldn't add to the show. But that's my own personality pressing on theirs. My assumption is always that they don't feel good enough to join in. The truth for many is perhaps the opposite – they are entirely at peace with watching something and not

250

being a part of it. This is the performer's curse – definitely the improviser's curse – anything I watch in theatre or TV, I immediately just want to be part of in some way.

I know the joy that comes from joining in with something, and I always want to encourage others to join in but that is sometimes more about me than about them. But when someone does feel included, and perhaps unusually so, and joins in with the game you're playing, and enjoys it, that is very nice.

The small things you do can have a big effect on someone. The 'I like your shoes' you muttered to someone in the street might make their day. The directions you gave a stranger might ease their day or inadvertently take them on the scenic route. Some music you recommended might become your friend's favourite new song and cause them to take up the guitar again. Seeing you strutting round showing off your lovely big bum might make someone else feel nice about their lovely big bum. The quick drunken snap you took at a party might be one of your friend's favourite ever photos and they actually print it and frame it. The server you were nice to at Pret might have dealt with a bevy of pricks all afternoon and you're a much-needed relief. Vice versa – the person you serve while you work at Pret might have dealt with a bevy of pricks all afternoon and you're a much-needed relief. Someone's reading the book you mentioned. Someone's eating the brownies you baked. Someone's laughing at the show you raved about. The white cot you gave away for free is being used (thank you). The orange jacket you handed over in a clothes swap is being worn (thank you). The WhatsApp message you left is being laughed at (thank you). The weekly gig you offered has made my year better (thank you). The prints you made for us in hospital are our best way of remembering her (thank you).

A piece of random advice you wrote might help someone write a book (thank you).

What's for you won't pass you #3
Or
Nap wherever you can

17 September 2021

This morning, I was up at 3.30am, 6am and 8am.
I have been vomited on twice.
I have poo on my dressing gown.
My tits hurt.
My head hurts.
I'm starving
and a demonic siren is going off inches from my head.

I am very lucky.

My beautiful boy arrived at teatime on a cold day at the end of July, all purple and covered in white goop. Summer never came this year – there was no heat, no sunny days. We kept thinking summer would arrive late, but it has passed us by completely. But our summer, our sunshine, came in the form of this little parcel. My seasons would now revolve around him.

From the moment he was handed to me, I couldn't quite believe he was mine. I can't believe I get to keep him. I know I'm biased but he is the best baby of them all and I'm sorry to the other mums who have other babies but this fact is obvious.

From the second he was born, he was constantly moving his arms and legs – just like he did in the womb. I recognised those big kicks, those furtive reaches. His tiny hands make gestures, patterns and signs in the air; sometimes like a wizard casting a spell, sometimes like a conductor leading a symphony, sometimes like a 90s raver dancing to the Prodigy. He looks mad. I love his mad little hands.

It is tiring, yes; I am so exhausted some days I literally can't move my face. Turns out there's very little difference between resting bitch face and knackered mum face. 'Nap whenever you can', this advice says. 'Nap when the baby naps', the books say. But it doesn't work – when they're awake you're looking after them with both hands, and when they're asleep you finally get time to eat, wee and possibly, as a luxury, wash. But washing's a rare treat and I am now resigned to constantly smelling of milk-vom, sweat and dry shampoo.

It's tiring, it's upsetting; when he cries for hours and it's just you and him, and you just want to help him and you can't help him except to keep holding him and telling him it's all right, and that he's safe and that you love him, all while mainlining paracetamol to stave off that migraine he's giving you.

It's tiring, it's upsetting, it's life-changing; I cried the most about not knowing how I would ever leave the house alone again, or how I would ever work, or travel, or write, or wear anything except sick-covered slacks and stained nursing bras that utterly failed to support my massive unwieldy boobs that didn't feel like mine anymore.

It is all those things and it is the best thing in the world. I have found the clichés to be true; it's the most difficult, most brilliant thing.

He smiled early. The books say that before two months they're not 'real smiles'. Well sorry, the books, but my boy smiled early and he keeps on smiling and it is real.

I wonder if he knows how much he is loved. I wonder if that seeps through somehow into their little heads. I wonder if he knows how wanted he is, and how happy he makes people.

People say he looks like his dad or like me or like his granddad or his cousin or his nephew half-removed, but I say he looks like himself. He just looks like a totally new person to me, which seems like a bit of magic. We made him, I grew him, but here he is and he's just himself – a brand new human.

We were given piles and piles of secondhand baby clothes from friends and family and one of the baby grows we were given has 'Little Miracle' on the front. I never liked that kind of cheesy branding around baby stuff. When I first saw it, before he was born, I thought it was mawkish. But I get it now. I saw him in it this morning and I thought, yeah there's something in that. He is a little miracle. But not from God. He's our miracle. I am his and he is mine. My baby, my boy, my Billy.

Prologue: You'll be fine

In the end, the powerful, inspirational and presumably-histori-cally-revered speech to my old school, the one that had set me off on this national quest for wisdom, was quite a simple one. Its message was about saying 'yes' to opportunities you might not have planned for, not setting your path too rigidly. It was a bit like the chapter 'Follow your dreams' but with more in-jokes about P.E. teachers and the canteen. There isn't time in one speech to cover every aspect of life from childbirth to pockets to macaron consumption.

But when it came to what I wanted to leave these girls with, I looked over all the advice I'd received and there was one unifying theme to most of it. It usually boiled down to something like 'You'll Be Fine'. So, I left them with that – I wrote a song called 'You'll Be Fine' and I sang it to them.

The words are below.*

You'll be fine. I promise that.
Things are scary at 11 or 18 (and 35)
But you'll be fine. Come good or bad.
Rain and shine, you will be fine, just wait and see
And not everything goes to plan
I'm sure the shit will hit the fan
And splurge back in your face I can
Just see it
But you're stronger than you think, I guarantee it

---

* If you'd like to hear the song, it's available in the audiobook. If you'd like to hear someone tell you that you'll be fine, you can tell yourself. I'd recommend it.

Get a cloth and wipe it off
And you'll be fine.

You'll be fine. You'll just do it.
And I don't mean that your dreams will all come true
They probably won't. But you'll think 'screw it'
Dreams are dreams and life is weird and so are you
It's good when, in real life, you fail,
Sometimes succeed, sometimes you nail it's
Better than a fairytale: it's all yours.
There's so much out there for you so open all doors
You will do it – just walk through it,
You'll be fine.

You'll be fine, I promise that
You'll fuck up, I mean *'your star will rise and fade'*
But like Kate Bush and like Take That
Get excited cos your comebacks will be great
You've got the world ahead of you
It's broadly getting better, too
So Do or Die – Decide on 'DO', just do it
Look for your life. And then pursue it.
Now get to it.
You'll. Be. Fine.

Acknowledgements

I'd like to thank the people who helped me write this book and some of the people who helped me in my life *while* I wrote this book.

Firstly, my brilliant editor, Myfanwy Moore. Thank you for giving me the opportunity to write at a time when I really needed to, for being patient when things got hard, and for your sensitivity and insight. Thank you Izzy Everington for all your hard work getting the book together and to the incredible team of women who have worked on different aspects of bringing it into the world; Alice Morley, Vero Norton, Jo Myler, Katie King and Karla Gowlett.

Thank you to my amazing friends who have supported, inspired and made me laugh and kept me (mostly) sane; the Hildabeasts, the Ladycunts, the Loughborough Lads, my dearest bonnets and Jess (Pinhead).

I want to thank my teachers over the years; those who taught me to read, to write, to act, to play, to listen, to think, to question and to persevere. I've had some really great teachers, and I think that makes me very lucky.

Thank you to those who contributed their expertise and experience to me for the book; Natasha Devon, Sophie Collins, Amy Cooke-Hodgson, and those whose writing was incredibly helpful and inspiring; Alex Holmes, Reni Eddo-Lodge, Laura Bates, Caitlin Moran, Caroline Criado-Perez, Gabby Edlin, Cariad Lloyd and Ellie Taylor.

Thanks to Loughborough High School, for asking me to give that speech. And for a great seven years back in the nineties!

Thanks to all the NHS staff in the maternity wards at St Thomas' hospital, from doctors to midwives to bereavement counsellors. Lucy, Anna, Jenny, Alex, Pooja, Amy, and so many more who were with me in the worst of times and the best of times. The work you do is so hard and I'll never forget it.

I want to thank my agent Sophie Chapman, for being an anchor, an ally and a friend.

Thank you to my live audiences. Thank you to those who came to see Keynote and gave me your advice. I hope you like what I did with it!

Thank you to Zarina for taking such good care of Billy while I finished this book.

Thanks to my mum and dad who are both, slightly secretly, very good at writing, and who brought me up to be creative, and to make things.

And thank you to Marcus. This book is wrapped around the life we've shared together the last few years. Thank you for making that life with me, for making me laugh, for letting me share your two lovely chumps, and giving me chump #5.

Notes

1. Hewitt, Rachel. 2019. 'I Decided to Start Walking down the Street like a Man. Spoiler: It Didn't Go Well.' *New Statesman*. September 6, 2019. https://www. newstatesman.com/politics/uk-politics/2019/09/i-decided-start-walking-down-street-man-spoiler-it-didn-t-go-well.

2. Roy, Jessica. 2015. 'What Happens When a Woman Walks Like a Man?' *The Cut*. January 8, 2015. https://www.thecut.com/2015/01/manslamming-manspreading-microaggressions.html.

3. 'Sidewalk Behaviour Exercise.' 2010. *Feminist Philosophers*. October 30, 2010. https://feministphilosophers.wordpress.com/2010/10/30/sidewalk-behaviour-exercise/.

4. Castrillon, Caroline. 2019. 'How Women Can Stop Apologizing and Take Their Power Back.' *Forbes*. July 15, 2019. https://www.forbes.com/sites/carolinecastrillon/2019/07/14/how-women-can-stop-apologizing-and-take-their-power-back/?sh=ad318064ce68.

5. Whippman, Ruth. 2019. 'Opinion: Enough Leaning In. Let's Tell Men to Lean Out.' *New York Times*. October 10, 2019. https://www.nytimes.com/2019/10/10/opinion/sunday/feminism-lean-in.html?smid=nytcore-ios-share.

6. Pretty Good Digital. 2019. 'Glastonbury Festival - Please Don't Pee on the Land.' Glastonbury Festival – 21st–25th June, 2017. 2019. https://www.glastonburyfestivals.co.uk/information/green-glastonbury/please-dont-pee-on-the-land/.

7. Gabriel, Michelle. 2020. 'Why Are Women's Pockets so Small? - *the Fact Shop*.' The Fact Shop. August 19, 2020. https://www.thefactshop.com/fashion-facts/why-are-womens-pockets-small.

8. 'WORLD'S USE OF POCKETS; Men's Clothes Full of Them, While Women Have but Few. CIVILIZATION DEMANDS THEM A Tailor Tells the Queer Purposes Pockets Are Made by Some Men to Fulfil.' *New York Times*. August 28, 1899. timesmachine.nytimes.com/timesmachine/1899/08/28/102534376.html?pageNumber=7.

9. Smith, Matthew. 2020. 'What Women Want: Pockets They Can Use.' Yougov.co.uk. YouGov. October 29, 2020. https://yougov.co.uk/topics/lifestyle/articles-reports/2020/10/29/what-women-want-pockets-they-can-use.

10. Alfonso, Fernando. 2020. 'Sports like Soccer Are Many of the Old Hobbies People Are Revisiting during the Pandemic. That Includes Brittany Boen in

Arizona.' *CNN*. April 5, 2020. https://edition.cnn.com/2020/04/05/world/old-hobbies-quarantine-coronavirus-wellness-trnd/index.html.

11.   Sweney, Mark. 2020. 'Britons Watched TV for 40% of Waking Hours during Covid Lockdown.' *Guardian*. August 4, 2020. https://www.theguardian.com/tv-and-radio/2020/aug/05/britons-tv-covid-lockdown-ofcom-streaming-netflix-amazon.

12.   Anderton, Joe. 2020. 'Sky History Axes Lee Mack Woodworking Reality Show Following Claims a Contestant Has Nazi Tattoos.' *Digital Spy*. October 20, 2020. https://www.digitalspy.com/tv/reality-tv/a34425694/sky-history-nazi-tattoos-lee-mack-the-chop/.

13.   Lord Ashcroft. 2015. 'The People, the Parties and the NHS - Lord Ashcroft Polls.' Lordashcroftpolls.com. January 14, 2015. https://lordashcroftpolls.com/2015/01/people-parties-nhs/.

14.   Dyan, Mark, and Nigel Edwards. 2017. 'Fact or Fiction? The NHS Has Too Many Managers.' The Nuffield Trust. January 16, 2017. https://www.nuffieldtrust.org.uk/news-item/fact-or-fiction-the-nhs-has-too-many-managers.

15.   Kanter, Jake. 2020. 'Meghan Markle Reveals She Suffered a Miscarriage in New York Times.' *Deadline*. November 25, 2020. https://deadline.com/2020/11/meghan-markle-suffered-miscarriage-new-york-times-1234621687/.

16.   O'Neill, Brendan. 2020. 'Do We Really Need to Know about Meghan Markle's Miscarriage?' Spiked-Online.com. Spiked. November 26, 2020. https://www.spiked-online.com/2020/11/26/do-we-really-need-to-know-about-meghan-markles-miscarriage/.

17.   Lehmiller, Justin. 2015. 'Why Men and Women Have Different Sexual Regrets.' *Psychology Today*. September 8, 2015. https://www.psychologytoday.com/gb/blog/the-myths-sex/201509/why-men-and-women-have-different-sexual-regrets.

18.   Dhrodia, Azmina. 2017. 'We Tracked 25,688 Abusive Tweets Sent to Women MPs – Half Were Directed at Diane Abbott.' *New Statesman*. September 5, 2017. https://www.newstatesman.com/science-tech/2017/09/we-tracked-25688-abusive-tweets-sent-women-mps-half-were-directed-diane-abbott.

19.   Elliott, Francis, and Janice Turner. 2017. 'MP Jess Phillips Forced to Filter Her Tweets after 600 Rape Threats in a Day.' *The Times*. August 25, 2017. https://www.thetimes.co.uk/article/mp-jess-phillips-forced-to-filter-her-tweets-after-600-rape-threats-in-a-day-6655nr57m.

20.   Wyatt, Daisy. 2014. 'Zoella: Zoe Sugg's Book Girl Online Becomes Fastest-Selling Debut Novel Ever.' *Independent*. December 3, 2014. https://www.

independent.co.uk/arts-entertainment/books/news/zoella-zoe-sugg-s-book-girl-online-becomes-biggestselling-debut-novel-ever-9898676.html.

21. Rahim, Zamira. 2019. 'Boris Johnson Showed "Disgracefully Cavalier" Attitude to Studies, School Letter Reveals.' *The Independent*. October 4, 2019. https://www.independent.co.uk/news/uk/politics/boris-johnson-rory-stewart-eton-college-letters-live-a9142711.html.

22. RNZ, "Prime Minister Jacinda Ardern statement to the nation on Covid-19, March 21," YouTube video, 8:31, March 21, 2020, https://www.youtube.com/watch?v=AvRuYrH5rjs.

23. Chesnut, J. 1968. *Woman Without Love*.

24. Kucynski, Alex, and William Glaberson. 2001. 'Book Author Says He Lied in His Attacks on Anita Hill in Bid to Aid Justice Thomas (Published 2001).' *New York Times*. June 27, 2001. https://www.nytimes.com/2001/06/27/us/book-author-says-he-lied-his-attacks-anita-hill-bid-aid-justice-thomas.html.

25. 'Jeremy Corbyn: "I Want a Kinder Politics."' *BBC News*. September 29, 2015. https://www.bbc.co.uk/news/av/uk-politics-34392427.

26. Vaughan, Richard. 2021. 'Voters May Raise an Eyebrow at Boris Johnson's Call for More "Kinder" Political Debate.' *Inews*. January 18, 2021. https://inews.co.uk/news/analysis/boris-johnson-political-debate-kind-civil-discourse-834246.

27. Iqbal, Nosheen. 2020. '#BeKind: Can Caroline Flack's Final Plea Be More than Just a Hashtag?' *Guardian*. February 22, 2020. https://www.theguardian.com/uk-news/2020/feb/22/caroline-flack-final-plea-be-kind-hashtag.

28. Davis, Barney. 2021. 'Influencer Sheridan Mordew Grilled on This Morning over Dubai Trip.' *Evening Standard*. January 26, 2021. https://www.standard.co.uk/news/uk/sheridan-mordew-dubai-influencer-this-morning-b901201.html.